As It Were

About the Author

Jonathan Biggins is an actor, writer, TV presenter and director of revue for the Sydney Theatre Company. His writing collaborations include an adaptation of *Orpheus in the Underworld*, a musical *The Republic of Myopia*, the revues *Sunday in Iraq With George* and *Stuff All Happens* and a regular column for *Good Weekend* magazine.

Born in Newcastle, NSW, he now lives in Sydney with his wife and twin daughters.

Jonathan Biggins

As It Were

A satirical and humorous look through history

ABC
Books

Published by ABC Books for the
AUSTRALIAN BROADCASTING CORPORATION
GPO BOX 9994 Sydney NSW 2001

First published March 2006

National Library of Australia
Cataloguing in Publication entry
Biggins, Jonathan.
As it were.
ISBN 0 7333 1531 3.

1. History - Humour. I. Australian Broadcasting Corporation.
II. Title.
909

Cover and internal design by Ellie Exarchos
Typeset by Ellie Exarchos in 10.5/15pt Adobe Garamond
Printed in Australia by Griffin Press, Netley, South Australia

2 4 5 3 1

To my Dad

Thanks to Elaine Smith, Fenella Souter, The *Good Weekend* subs, Jill Brown, Geraldine Corridon and Jody Lee.

History is a gallery of pictures in which
there are few originals and many copies
Alexis de Tocqueville 1805-59

Plus ça change, plus c'est la même chose
French — look it up

Contents

7,896,426,586 BC

The creation
of the universe

In the beginning, God created a committee. Then he fashioned a small room where they could assemble, with tea- and coffee-making facilities (cold drinks at an additional charge) and a Gestetner machine for the minutes. The first meeting began at ten minutes past the dawn of time and it was decided to select the chair by a show of hands. Unfortunately, God hadn't got around to creating light, so nobody could see the hands and there was a bit of a hold-up before the celestial bodies started glowing with a thin humming noise.

And lo, there sat all the gods and demi-gods, blinking in the strange pale dawn. There sat the deities of Olympus; the Norse and Teutonic gods, proud and warrior-like; the Eastern heavenly beings; the pagan guardians of hearth and home; Satan and the angels; the Hindu gods; the deities of the ancient Persians and Phoenicians; the spirits of the Dreamtime and a small god named Steve, who represented the soon-to-be-lost religion of the dinosaurs.

God himself, wearing a name tag to avoid confusion,

emerged from behind a cloud and sat at the head of the table. 'Energy-saving orbs; I'm afraid they'll take a bit of time to warm up. Right. Well, thank you all for coming. Let's make a start: first item on the agenda.'

'Shouldn't we read the minutes of the last meeting?' said a woodland sprite, representing the northern pagans.

'I don't see how we can, seeing this is the first meeting we've ever had. First meeting in history, as a matter of fact,' said God.

'And I daresay it won't be the last,' remarked Apollo.

'Quite. Anyway, there's a lot to plough through so let's get on with it. Now, I'm the temporary chairgod, of course, but who—apart from myself—wants to nominate for the permanent position?'

Satan, wearing a T-shirt saying 'I Love Lucifer' and waiting for the right moment to slip a whoopee cushion onto Pluto's chair, immediately volunteered. A few other arms rose tentatively; Zeus and one or two of the Eastern mystics.

'Marvellous!' said God, scarcely disguising his displeasure behind a distant rumble of peevishness. 'As I mentioned earlier, we'll do this on a show of hands. You Hindu deities: one hand at a time, please.'

It was a close-run thing, but finally God edged out Satan in a recount.

'Better luck next time, Prince of Darkness,' said God cheerfully. 'Would you like to be social secretary?'

'Sounds brilliant,' said Satan with the easy graciousness of one long accustomed to losing.

'Splendid! Let's kick off with a progress report on the creation of the universe. Mercury, if you'd do the honours?'

The Roman god of couriers stood up and walked to the flip-chart, adjusting his toga nervously and scratching one winged ankle against the other.

'Thank you, God—and can I just say what a great

opportunity it is to be working with you, this is so going to look cool on my CV! Okay, right. Creation of the universe. Ah, good news is we are on track. Big bang went off without a hitch, dust clouds now starting to slowly form galaxies, although I'd have to say we weren't counting on anti matter. One or two stars already about but the latest indications have us looking at planet formation in two or three million years.'

'So soon?' said the August Personage of Jade. 'That is but the brush of a marten's wing against the granite mountain as she flies south for the winter.'

'What the hell is a marten?' said Hermes.

'Didn't you get my memo? You know—it was about that form we all got asking for suggestions for what we should put on the earths. I've had an idea for these things called birds and a marten is …'

'I think we're getting a little ahead of ourselves,' said God, 'but August has brought us to the next item of business. Did you all get the forms he mentioned? Splendid. Now I have a suggestion: I really think we should just create the one earth, a trial run, if you will. Find a spot for it somewhere in the universe and try out a few ideas. So today's meeting, really, is all about what we do with it — do we have water? How much grass do we want to put down, should there be leeches, that sort of thing.'

'What will we have to work with?'

'Mind if I jump in here, God?' asked Mercury. 'The one earth will probably be a molten core surrounded by a mantle of rock.'

'Then there must be little rocks for throwing!' bellowed Mars. 'And pointy sticks for smiting and stabbing! Thunderrr!'

'Hang on a minute, Mars … little rocks,' said God, writing as fast as he could.

'And pointy sticks …'

'For the smiting and the stabbing, okay, I'm with you now.'

'Who, or what, is going to be doing the stabbing?' asked Jupiter.

'Good point,' said God. 'If I could bring you into the loop, August Personage, is this something that could tie in with your bird idea?'

'Um … I wasn't thinking of a stabbing bird but maybe the bird could have little sharp sticks in its feet, that might work. And maybe it could use those to hunt for food.'

'Food?'

'Yes, food. To make it live,' said the AP of Jade.

'Hang on a second, I'm confused here,' said Satan. 'Are you saying that whatever we put on the one earth won't be like us and simply *exist*? Are you saying these things will have to live and then … stop living? Do we have a word for that?'

'I have a word!' cried Mars. 'Die, mortal, die!'

'Bugger,' said Ahura Mazda. 'I was going to use that word for a six-sided device in a game of chance.'

'Satan raises a very important issue,' said God. 'I don't think we want any more eternal beings, we've already duplicated quite a few portfolios — no offence intended, Zeus and Jupiter. But I like this notion of creatures that simply stop. However, what happens to them after that?'

'Could they come back as something else?'

'Yes — to die again!' shouted Mars.

'Recycling, that's a very positive suggestion. Or perhaps a select few could join us in heaven,' said God.

'Might get a bit crowded. How many are we thinking of?'

'Pluto and I could always take a few off your hands,' said Satan.

'Yes, so you could,' said God, warming to the idea. 'I like the concept of a heaven and a hell — something to aspire to and something to run from, that should keep them guessing. But getting back to AP's other point about food, well, that just opens a whole new can of worms.'

'Worms being ... ?' asked Woden.

'You know, I've never given that much thought. But I'll have a go. Worms are ... er ... small, little tubes that live in the ground and eat very, very small rocks, so small in fact that they're no longer rocks but something called ... er ... soil! I say, this is rather fun!'

'And will the worms be joining us in heaven?'

'Oh, I shouldn't think so. I think we're after a slightly higher class of creation than that. Perhaps they could be food for AP's birds! And speaking of sustenance, I think we could all do with a short refreshment break—not that we need it of course, but who doesn't love the taste? Venus, Artemis—perhaps you'd be so kind as to fetch in the coffee and a few pastries?'

'Why us?' asked Venus pointedly.

'Well, goddesses are just better at that sort of thing,' said God, a little flustered, looking around the table for support. With the exception of Mars, every deity was pointedly gazing out through imaginary windows, leaving God to flounder alone. 'Oh, alright,' he finally grumbled. 'Take Bacchus and Hermaphrodite with you—but don't touch the executive fridge, Bacchus. I've drawn a line on the gin bottle, I know exactly how much is left.'

Clutching their hot beverages and one allotted pastry (God being something of a penny pincher), the heavenly creatures scattered into break-out groups to workshop ideas for igneous rocks, tundra, the hapless wildebeest and other pressing earth creation issues. Mercury wandered about the room with a sheaf of Reflection Matrix forms, which the gods filled in and handed back to Calliope and Urania, who collated the data and compiled a series of overhead transparencies. After half an hour—or two thousand earth years—God rang a little bell and everyone drifted back to the table.

Turning down the celestial orbs, God projected the transparencies, nodding in approval as the stage one concept plan was gradually revealed. 'I very much like what I'm seeing,' he said. 'The flora and fauna division solves a lot of problems—I could never envisage just how bracken was going to be able to speak, but that's solved the conundrum nicely. I'm also quite taken with the stratification of the animal kingdom, I do love a good hierarchy, as you know. And moss! Never would have thought of that myself, well done, the Buddhists! Now, I think we can safely leave the details to one or two sub committees but we really should look a little more closely at the higher order of beings—what did you call them, Terpsichore? Woman, was it?'

'Well, that's a blanket term for both sexes if we go with the yin and yang suggestion.'

'I can't see a problem with that, they should rub along together quite easily. But "Woman" is a bit of a mouthful—I think it's best if we shorten it to "Man",' said God, quickly moving on before Venus could get a word in. 'First question is, what is Man going to look like?'

'The paragon of animals, a reflection of his or her creator,' said Juno.

'What—ten heads and twenty arms like Rakshasa? Winged like Mercury, or horned like Satan?' asked God.

'From what I've heard about Satan, I wouldn't say no to that!' said Aphrodite with a lewd wink.

God frowned in disapproval; he disliked innuendo. In fact he disliked a lot of things and behind his back was considered rather dull and old-fashioned.

'This might sound a bit pedantic,' said Steve, whose sole contribution to proceedings thus far had been to suggest a race of enormous creatures that'd be wiped out by a meteor shower. 'But what will Man himself think he looks like? Will he see himself as the mirror of divinity, or will he believe the zebra was made in the image of god?'

'I think you've just invented lateral thinking, Steve,' said God admiringly.

'More to the point,' said Ishtar, sounding worried, 'will he believe in any of us — or all of us? There are only so many hours in a day to worship the heavens.'

'Twenty-three to be exact,' chipped in Mercury, 'if we go with the current proposal.'

'It's a puzzling question,' mused God. 'Do we want Man to believe in us at all? What would be the point?'

'Well, if Man is going to aspire to heaven as a reason to get up in the morning, he'll have to at least believe in the existence of a landlord, or someone with a key to let him into paradise.'

'That's all very good for Man but what do we get out of it?' said Zeus. 'I've got better things to do with my time than hang about answering questions for a Man who thinks I'm a zebra.'

'Aren't we getting off the track here?' said Pluto. 'Why don't we just put the basic infrastructure in and see what evolves? And if it gets too much, we can always split the place into zones, each take care of a bit.'

'Seems reasonable,' said God approvingly. 'I must say I had no idea it would be so complicated. Maybe I should have just made this universe like all the others.'

There was a chorus of disagreement.

'I suppose you're right, have to think outside the comfort zone. And it's been marvellous to have your feedback. Very well, I'll have Mercury send you all the minutes and we'll wait and see what the sub committees come up with. If you could just leave your Attributes of Man suggestions with me, I'll have a bit of a think about that, but otherwise, well done with everybody.'

The supreme beings stood up and slowly made their way out, excitedly chatting and swapping ideas. God collected their Attributes of Man forms, and having said goodbye to the last of them, destroyed the crockery to save washing up, switched off the orbs and closed the door.

And in the darkness, Satan's whoopee cushion hid a tiny piece of paper bearing Steve's suggestion for mankind, two simple words that were lost for all time: Common Sense.

29,846 BC

Gogs of the
Stone Age

Once upon an ancient time, the prehistoric town of Gog lay nestled by a peat bog; an unassuming little cluster of cave dwellings and a flimsy lath-and-daub lean-to, thrown up by a speculative Neanderthal hoping for a quick sale to someone looking for an alfresco living-space right in the heart of the village atmosphere. So far the offer had been declined, most people preferring the warmth and relative dryness of the more traditional cave. Although when the harsh winter kept everyone inside for weeks on end even the pigs got touchy about the smell.

The village of Magog, another unassuming little cluster of cave dwellings, was about a day's lope south—the lope was the standard Goggian unit of distance, the smallest measurable length being the demi-lope, which made haute couture very difficult; hemlines were either a round the throat or trailing in the mud. Magog boasted a fine collection of ornamental dung jewellery, housed in the hollow of a tree and untouched since Zort had worn it for a few sun-ups then come out in a strange rash and expired.

All was not well in Gog. The economy was stagnating, perhaps not surprising given that the economy was based solely on cutting up the peat bog, but Goggians didn't fully understand the bog/stagnation symbiosis and had started to panic. They decided to form the Committee of Gog, a group of eminent cave-persons who could advance the town by generating lucrative initiatives. Splorg opened the meeting in the traditional way by urinating on the Social Secretary. (Some years later, when they were finding it hard to get anyone to nominate for Social Secretary, the custom was amended to urinating on the agenda.)

'Me declare meeting open. Gog in heapum economic trouble. Must beat Magog—get major events to raise profile.'

'Oh for goodness' sake, what is so difficult about pronouns and prepositions?' asked Thorg exasperatedly. Thorg was quite sophisticated; he'd changed his name from Forg and wore his pelts at a jaunty angle. 'We are not apes, so can we please stop gibbering like them!'

Splorg was miffed—some of his family technically still were apes. They all sat in thoughtful silence, tiny brains grinding away as their appendixes secreted soothing nicotine every twenty minutes—that's what appendixes did in those days, apparently. Then Quorg stood up, a squat chap with one eyebrow. He'd rashly attended the birth of his first child and his wife had bitten the other eyebrow off during labour. 'We take leaf from Magog's book,' he said. 'Tour exhibition of dung jewellery.' He raised his eyebrow and everyone assumed he was being deliciously ironic so they chuckled politely and moved on.

'I say we go for the Gay Games,' said Thorg. 'Let's put the *homo* into *homo erectus*.'

Splorg groaned. 'Look what happened with Mardi Gras. Complete disaster.'

'Well, it would've helped if someone had invented the wheel! What kind of procession just sits there?'

'Thorg, please,' said Splorg patiently. 'Me respect your lifestyle choice but we need something for mums and dads.'

'What about reality programme? Put people in cave, other people sit around and watch every move,' suggested Borg, former Gog–Magog District singles champion five years running.

'Nothing different from ordinary life—where is hook?' asked Dorg, who still lived with seventeen in-laws. 'We need to double population, be part of Asia.'

'What is Asia?' asked Quorg.

'Haven't foggiest,' replied Dorg 'but always sounds like good idea. Or maybe us build big new cave where us can shout, wave arms about and throw mud.'

'What is name of that?' asked Splorg.

'Parliament.'

'Man in street no care for that,' snorted Splorg. 'And Gog no need more white elephants.'

'But last white elephant tasted good and bones made excellent stock,' said Borg.

'That's it!' squealed Thorg. 'Let's have a Food Fair! Gog's top chefs using the finest produce from local growers.'

'What is grower?'

'Well alright, local hunters and gatherers, whatever. We can have stalls, vouchers and peat wine …'

'Family fun day?' ventured Quorg.

'Adults only,' said Thorg flatly—he'd long ago decided that art would be his only passport to immortality. 'We need a venue. Let's knock down the lean-to, build a convention centre and maybe even a casino!'

The committee looked doubtful. 'Mmm … cost too much money,' said Splorg with an air of finality.

Thorg refused to give up. 'Money? The local unit of currency is dried cow dung, for heaven's sake!'

'Only got one cow. Mustn't put pressure on monetary supply.'

'Typical!' muttered Thorg as he angrily gathered his things into a rather fetching tote bag made from a mastodon's scrotum. 'You've all got the vision of a blind man during a solar eclipse!' And he swept out of the cave in a dramatic gesture.

In the silence that followed Quorg raised his eyebrow. 'Well, who got out of animal-pelt pile on wrong side this morning?'

Some weeks later, Thorg absentmindedly twiddled a lump of chalk in his hand as he contemplated the empty Specials board. Having recently introduced café society into Gog, he felt duty-bound to keep his fellow Goggians abreast of the latest culinary developments. He'd even travelled to Magog to pick up a few innovative decor tips (cesspit *outside* the main dining area, that sort of thing) but frankly their menus were positively pre-Cambrian—they were still doing focaccias! Still, he knew the food game was a balancing act between innovation and tradition, especially when half his clientele still viewed eating the other half as perfectly acceptable. So mud and acorn pasties had to be offered for the diehards while he struggled to expand their horizons with brioche drizzled with a lemon myrtle jus. Sometimes he wondered why he bothered.

At a rustic table, perched on a colourful mismatched rock, his only customer for the week suspiciously eyed a friand. Borg was a confirmed bachelor who regularly dined out; in fact, he pretty much lived out, only digging a shallow ditch to lie in when the winter nights dropped below zero, which probably explained his marital status. A friand was news to him and at this point he was still trying to work out how something that cost so much could be so small. Thorg interrupted his rumination with an elaborate sigh.

'You know, Borg, I realise I'm the only *homo sapiens* in this one-bog town thinking about the future and I know it's early days but I'd have to say café society is not panning out exactly as I'd hoped. It's hardly your hub of conversation, is it? Where are the bohemians arguing about philosophy? Where are the idiosyncratic regulars dropping in for a pastis as they rapidly sketch on a napkin an image that will change the face of art for ever? All I get are philistines wanting French vanilla cordial in their ghastly mugaccinos!'

Borg remained silent. He knew for a fact that Thorg made cappuccino by farting repeatedly in a flat white and he dreaded to think what passed for the French vanilla cordial.

'What happened to the fiery exchange of ideas, the cut and thrust of debate? All people do these days is sit in their caves and bitch about each other. In this town, exercising your intellect is rated just under contracting genital warts as a good way of passing the time.'

Well, mused Borg inwardly, that really depended on how you contracted the warts in the first place … and anyway, Thorg knew as well as he did that intellectuals had always been thin on the ground in Gog. This was a place where walking upright for three consecutive days was considered an achievement.

'Maybe voices of dissent silenced by social climate,' he ventured through a spray of almond meal.

'You got dat right, sister!' agreed Thorg, who'd also recently introduced jive talkin' into Gog. 'You know who I blame?'

Borg quickly ran through the long list of Thorg's usual scapegoats in his mind.

'We're on the losing side of a culture war, my friend. Relaxed and comfortable battlers! Hello? Surely the terms are mutually exclusive! And all this rubbish about rewriting history—how ironic is that? We're pre historic to begin with! It was bad enough that your post modernists thought truth was a subjective construct—now the bloody thing doesn't even exist! And say what you like about the fascists but at least they told you to think something! No, the only brains Goggians admire are the ones chargrilled on sticks!'

Having little idea what Thorg was talking about, Borg waited patiently until his feisty friend had run out of exclamation marks. 'Maybe you should travel to new town?'

'What, after all the money I've sunk into this place? You have no idea how expensive furniture that uncomfortable is. I've spent three hundred byirts on the letterbox leaflet drops alone, God knows why, seeing as only five people in this miserable dump can read. But when the going gets tough, the tough stay put. I can see off the bad times, don't you worry. Nothing lasts for ever—look at the Ice Age.'

There was an awkward silence. Thorg decided to belatedly play the gracious host. 'So, how did you find the friand?'

'Me looked under little finger and there it was,' said Borg with a sheepish grin.

Thorg laughed in spite of himself. It was hardly a joke off the top shelf but in this day and age, he thought, any port in a storm.

Six months later, everything had changed. Well, the peat bog was still there and Gog had sunk another demi-semi-lope into it, but now the air was charged with the acrid stench of a constitutional crisis. Politics had recently been introduced to the simple inhabitants by a strange traveller from across the mountains, who'd arrived with a clipboard and some multiple-choice questions about issues that mattered. Unfortunately personal hygiene and Borg's reflux problem had not been listed as issues that mattered, so the Goggians could contribute little to the survey.

But the notion of an elected legislature was tantalising and within three moons, mayoral elections had been held. Suddenly Thorg's café became a hang-out for the new power elites, a place to be seen. And never more than when Splorg, the newly elected mayor (or CEO as he liked to fashion himself), was embroiled in a scandal that threatened the very office itself.

The details remain hazy to this day, diary keeping not being a Goggian strong suit, but apparently Dorg was shown some cave paintings that ostensibly cast, shall we say, a moral shadow on Zorg's wife, and he told Quorg, who relayed the information to someone in Splorg's department who briefed the CEO who then used the allegations for political advantage. Scarcely one sun-up later, Dorg was denying all knowledge of the incident and it looked like Splorg had very much put his foot in his mouth—in a metaphorical sense, as opposed to when he did it to clean out his toe nails.

Splorg's office went into damage control mode but the crisis escalated when Quorg revealed the chronology of events, a somewhat elastic sequence due to the lack of timekeeping devices, but nonetheless, a cynical public demanded an explanation. Thorg, considering himself Gog's master of spin-doctoring (a recently discovered application of the wheel), saw an opening and presented himself at Splorg's electoral cave.

'But how can me help?' asked Splorg worriedly.

'I've done it all, Splorg,' said Thorg, sweeping the office for bugs. He found two and ate them. 'Food and beverage, hospitality. As a celebrity hairdresser I perfected the dragged-through-a-hedge-backwards look for A-list socialites. I've dabbled in new media—who was the first using ochre? And I predicted bronze eons before anyone else! But right now I'm specialising in public image rightsizing. First things first. Total media embargo.'

Not a tall order, seeing Gog's fourth estate ran to Storg, who hosted a chat show in his cave, and Vorg, who carved satirical figurines out of antelope stools.

'But media my lifeblood!' protested Splorg. 'How me speak to people? To battlers?'

'Appallingly, as usual—that's not going to change, it gives you the common touch. But we set the parameters. No doorstops, no press conferences and if anyone asks the direct question, you don't hear it.'

'What question?'

'Exactly. Either that or you don't remember.'

'Remember what?' asked Splorg, protruding forehead wrinkled in concentration.

'Now you're getting the hang of it. You see, old news is no news. The press get bored long before you do, so you could sleep with a goat ...'

'What wrong with that?'

'Fair enough, bad example but my point is you can ride out anything.'

Splorg paced the floor. 'Me no like this. Me pro-active leader, sitting on hands not my style.'

You could put your feet on your hands and still stay upright, thought Thorg, but he smiled brightly and set some goals. 'Alright. Let's show Gog the real Splorg—do you have family? Anyone close?'

'Er ... you know goat you spoke of earlier?'

'Okay. New approach. Divert and distract. You go on a trade mission to Magog and if anyone brings this incident up, you say you weren't advised by your department.'

'Who going to believe that?'

'Trust me on this one,' chuckled Thorg. 'You tell the same

lie three times and everyone believes it.'

'That true?'

'Certainly is.'

'Three times?'

'Count 'em. Three.'

'Okay, me believe you. Only trouble is, me have no department. All sacked in last round of budget cuts.'

'But you draw a secretary's allowance … don't tell me, it's the goat, isn't it?' Splorg nodded guiltily. 'Well, I hope she takes good shorthand.'

'Er … he.'

Thorg could feel the situation rapidly moving beyond him. 'Alright,' he sighed. 'We're going to have to go with the absolute last line of defence.'

'What that?'

'Attack!'

———

Thorg hastily convened an assembly of Gog's finest minds then added a few more to make up the numbers. As a cunning diversion, he called the meeting to ostensibly discuss the village's disastrous move from hunter-gathering to agriculture. Quorg's coriander had failed completely and Dorg's rocket crop couldn't have fed a rabbit, so with primitive logic they'd eaten the rabbit instead.

'Let's face it,' said Thorg. 'Salad greens are completely beyond us. We need another value-added product pronto or Gog misses the global boat.' He nudged Splorg's elbow but Splorg simply looked at him blankly. 'I think our CEO has a few words to say,' continued Thorg, kicking Splorg vigorously in the shin.

'Splorg lame-duck leader under scandal cloud,' said Dorg.

'Even so, he has valuable ideas to contribute, don't you?' hinted Thorg.

A byirt dropped in the distant recesses of Splorg's brain and he struggled to his feet. 'Maybe we can export intellectual property to address balance of trade ...' he said slowly. Thorg was stunned—even he hadn't thought of that—and it was the most coherent sentence Splorg had ever strung together. But the immense cerebral effort had fused his nascent language receptors and he spent the rest of the meeting dribbling in the corner. Thorg sighed and turned to the others: Dorg, Quorg, two gibbons and a relatively smart dog.

'What Splorg was hoping to say was that if we miss the global boat ...'

'What is global boat?' asked Dorg.

'It's the future, the only way off the bottom of the dung heap. You want to get Gog noticed? You want to be something in this world?'

'What is world?' ventured Quorg.

'You know, the other side of the mountains, beyond the forest. I've been there and let me tell you, no-one—and I mean no-one—has ever heard of Gog.'

Quorg and Dorg looked at each other apprehensively. Apart from a long weekend in Magog, they had never ventured beyond the peat bog and felt inadequate next to a cosmopolitan sophisticate like Thorg. He had journeyed far and had introduced the spfort, a tasteless berry that had become their staple breakfast food until Jorg had discovered continental-style yoghurt.

'Maybe we not want world to hear,' murmured Dorg, the gibbons nodding in agreement.

'Are you crazy?' said Thorg. 'I've got two caves full of spforts that I've got to move by the end of the month and the local market's collapsed. We need trade and we need it now.'

'Why not we sell to Magog?'

'Hello? If we're the bottom of the dung heap, Magog's the

dirt the heap's sitting on! No, Gog needs friends at the top, so I say we start making them. And they don't come any more top-like than … Attadungog!'

Quorg, Dorg and the gibbons gasped, all thoughts of constitutional crisis forgotten. Attadungog! Even they had heard of the all-conquering village of powerful warriors, far off to the east, who held the wheel patent and drank red wine with fish. They were the stuff of legend.

'Why Attadungog want to be friends with Gog?' asked Dorg.

'Well, I've heard it through the grapevine that they're preparing for war with Welliamagog,' said Thorg with an air of self-importance.

Dorg had to hand it to Thorg; the grapevine tightly strung between two half-gourds had worked just as he'd said it would—it was amazing, it was as if the person you were talking to was in the same cave.

'So I propose,' Thorg continued, 'that Gog sends our army off to pre-empt their pre-emptive strike! The Attadungoggians will love us!'

The gibbons looked positively alarmed. They were in the army reserve; hell, they *were* the army reserve but they'd only done it for the free bananas and the bivouacs! Going to war? They started hooting and slapping the walls in dismay.

'But army not ready, still waiting on review of external threat,' stammered Quorg. 'And I have a cousin in Welliama-gog—they not all bad.'

'Well, if you want to play in the big league you've got to break a few eggs,' shrugged Thorg. Metaphors were a new thing in Gog and there were still the occasional teething problems. 'When the going gets tough, the lark ascends.'

The others had no idea what he was talking about—the dog had given up long ago—but they were worried by Thorg's odd behaviour. He'd started drawing attack plans in the sand and sharpening sticks.

'We've got to be prepared to stand by our allies. Who knows what evil lurks in Welliamagog? They're crazy people! Do you want to say to your children, "I had the chance but I did nothing"?'

Dorg was silent. Finally Quorg murmured, 'If that how you feel, Thorg. You know best. Now that Splorg is vegetable lame-duck leader under scandal cloud, we obey you. You lead us to war, we follow.'

Thorg stopped dead. 'Me? You're saying *I* should go to war?'

'Well, you commander-in-chief now and if you no go, that only leave five and gibbons.'

'Hey, guys!' blustered Thorg. 'I'm just tossing ideas around here, come on! There's more than one way to skin a melon. Okay, okay, let's forget the war thing. How's about we send a folkloric dance troupe out on tour instead?'

435 BC

The birth
of democracy

As Bartonocrates strode triumphantly into the party room, the newly elected elders rose as one, wildly applauding the first democratically elected Prime Minister of the Athenian city-state. The Corinthian scratch band of musicians seated uncomfortably in the corner hastily ended their bracket of epic poetry set to the lyre and began a noisy march of celebration with much banging of the tabor and blowing of the horn. It had been a long and stressful night for the party faithful—four messengers alone had dropped dead after bringing in the latest figures from the tally-room in Marathon—and news of the great victory had swept over them all with a surge of relief. Bartonocrates ascended the dais and, with a self-effacing wave of his hands, brought the ovation to an end.

'Thank you, friends and colleagues. This is as much a victory for democracy as it is for me. Even though the majority of people said it wouldn't work, well, they were wrong, and I think the figures that came in from the booths scattered throughout the land from Delphi to Mycenae—and from our fellow Athenians serving overseas in Troy—prove that a just and equitable electoral system will be here for as long as the gods themselves. I've always been a great believer in the common sense of the Athenian people, the battlers in small businesses from anchovies to amphorae, the farmers in the groves—the most efficient farmers anywhere in the known world, I might add—but can I just say this: at the end of the day, the sun goes down. We accept this victory proudly, yet with great humility. Gods bless Athens!'

The faithful again leapt to their feet. Castor and Demeraras, heirs to the sugar fortune and dynamic fund raisers; Tarmax, the newly elected member for Rhodes; Taramas Alata, the artist who'd designed the hand bills—even Dubious the Cynic managed a muted 'Hear! Hear!' before thinking better of it. This was history in the making and all present were humbled by the knowledge that they would be the first men in history to receive a parliamentary pension. Basking with civic pride and a recognition of the contribution they could make to society, they revelled in a spirit of elation that would only be punctured by the invention of the political journalist.

Paraxetemol, Minister for Health elect, quipped: 'Hey, Bartonocrates—it's half an hour since the count was declared. You're now the longest-serving prime minister ever!'

The laughter was broken by the gloomy voice of Filofax, party secretary. 'I'm afraid the honeymoon's over,' he said flatly. 'The next election campaign started yesterday.'

'But we've only had one quaff of ambrosia and the souvlaki's not even cooked!' complained Porxalot, corpulent representative of the Bacchus Marsh electorate.

'This isn't the time for complacency—we've got to get back out there and start listening. Citizens are hurting,' said Filofax with a peevish glare of disapproval. 'Our research shows we're out of touch with the aspirational voters in the western Peloponnese.'

'Already?' asked Bartonocrates incredulously. 'That was quick!'

Filofax shrugged. 'A new moon is a long time in politics. I've been exit polling the lads down at the gymnasium …'

'Who hasn't?' said someone.

Filofax ignored the interjector. 'Now *we* know we won on sound management of the drachma, don't we?' He scanned the room to make sure they'd all read the press releases. 'But what *they* don't know is that we've got about as much control over the market as the sand has over the sea.'

'What market are you talking about? The olive market on a Thursday? Or the Friday fish and pre loved homewares?' asked Tarmax.

'The only market that counts: the big wide world of economics. That's what your voters care about.'

'Economix? I'm pretty sure I went to school with a guy called Economix. Last I heard, he'd run off with a Macedonian,' said Porxalot, basting the yiros and pouring himself another honeyed wine.

Filofax shook his head in despair. Already the councillors had gravitated into clusters of like-minded souls; the military clique in one corner were light-heartedly forming a phalanx, the philosophy enthusiasts contemplated the essence of a dolmade in another, and out on the balcony, the theatre-lovers were deconstructing the latest work of Aeschylus— 'And he has the nerve to call that a comedy? I know comedy, and I can tell you, a man with no arms could've counted the laughs on one hand.' And so the factional system was born. It had been hard enough to unite this bickering, incompetent rabble of egos into a disciplined team for the election campaign; the thought of them governing Athens was more than Filofax could embrace. Perhaps a second assembly of review was needed, or maybe they could all be sacked and a tyrant—no, an interim administrator—be appointed. Now there's a thought, he thought, pulling out his slate and jotting down a note to self.

'The truth is,' he said to those who were still listening as he clipped away his stylus, 'there's a backlash against the Aegean Solution. We've got to rethink our strategy in the marginals; you can only play the Trojan vote once.'

Bartonocrates wasn't so sure. He was a canny judge of the Athenian character, and when the galley filled with women and children fleeing the war in Troy had sailed over the horizon, he'd recognised it for the golden opportunity it was. He knew his fellow citizens were far more worried about foreigners than they were about tariff reductions on sandals.

'Why don't we go for the Lesbians?' he suggested. 'No-one likes them either. Can't we stick all of them on an island as well?'

'Trouble is, they're already on an island.'

'Could we drown them?'

'That's a sound policy initiative and the sort of bold reform that many would admire but I really think it's a second-or third-term agenda,' said Filofax. 'We need to broaden our voter base in the interim.'

'What about women?' asked Porxalot.

Heads turned to him in disbelief. 'You want to put *women* on the electoral role?' asked Filofax, aghast.

'Gods no!' said Porxalot hurriedly. 'I was just thinking, if this is going to be a long meeting, maybe we should order some now.'

'Good idea. I'll have a large Sicilian. Back to the electoral strategy. I think we need to present a minimal target: we mustn't reveal any of our policies.'

'Well that shouldn't be too hard—we haven't got any! We've only been in power for half an hour!' snorted Bartonocrates.

'Thirty-five minutes, actually—you've already broken your

own record as the longest-serving Prime …'

'Yes, thank you, Paraxetemol, we get the point.'

'Can't we do something positive to encourage voter support? Dangle a few carrots?' asked Geriatrix, minister-elect for Aged Care.

'Carrots are for donkeys,' said Filofax. 'Sure, your average Con-Blon in the agora is greedy for a little bit more but believe me, he's far more afraid of losing what he's already got. We've got to push the fear buttons.'

'But the 3 000 drachmas we gave for the cultural centre in the swinging seat of Nanamaskouri, that must have won us a few votes,' said Tarmax.

'Oh, sure. I'm not saying we don't drop a bit of honey every now and then but we've got to take the gloves off. People want a tough leader, someone who believes in traditional values and won't be swayed by fashionable ideas.'

'Like a man lying only with his wife?'

'Exactly—that's the kind of new fangled crap we've got to knock on the head. And here's another thing you do: target the Leader of the Opposition…'

'The leader of the what?'

'The Opposition. It's kind of the downside of democracy; just under half of you are supposed to diametrically oppose everything the others suggest.'

'But why?' asked a puzzled Paradox. 'We've all been equally elected, why can't we just discuss the issues and make a collective decision?'

Filofax gave a world-weary smile. 'A word of advice, my friend. This is a real man's world. Welcome to the bearpit, a cauldron of intrigue where the strong rise triumphant, slavering over the carcasses of the slain.'

'I thought that was the half-price meat-lover's buffet at Theo's Taverna!' quipped the irrepressible Paraxetemol.

'All those in favour of Paraxetemol being Leader of the Opposition?' asked Bartonocrates. Every hand in the room but one shot skyward.

'And once you're in that bearpit,' said Filofax, 'every second of every minute of every hour you've got to be figuring out the way to stay on top. It's not the governing that's important; it's being in government.'

'Hang on,' said a worried Paraxetemol. 'Don't I get a turn in government?'

'Stick around long enough and everyone gets a turn.'

Bartonocrates' eyes darted around the room like a cornered rodent. 'So what else should I do to stay in power?'

'Isolate your minorities, pump more money into the Olympics, get the medea on side—probably not a bad idea to stack the board of the Oracle of Delphi, we need some feel-good prophesies. Oh, and send a few guys to attack Sparta; war is votes on a plate.'

'OK. I'll give a million drachmas for hurdles, monotheists will be exiled, Murdox can have the next casino licence, the navy sails on the morning tide and Paraxetemol, Deputy Leader of the Opposition …'

'Deputy? Since when?'

'You were rolled in caucus. The opposition's in disarray, and you shall appear before the anti-corruption commission.'

'What did I do?'

'I have no idea but I'll think of something. I know—you rorted your travel allowance! How's that?'

'You're getting the hang of it,' said Filofax, smiling malevolently. 'Only one more thing—while you're on a roll, call the next election tomorrow.'

52 BC

Caesarean section

Through the mist that swirled and clung to the valley like a valley-clinging, swirling mist, the repetitive clatter of hobnailed sandals striking flagstones rang out. 'I don't know but I've been told!' chanted a disembodied voice in melodic sing song, straining to make itself heard above the noise. The phrase was immediately echoed in unison by a choir of phantoms. 'Vestal virgins are mighty cold!' answered the voice, the refrain taken up again by lusty throats with the odd lewd guffaw.

Wraith-like, from the suddenly parting fog, emerged the IVth Cohort of the XIIIth Roman Legion in all its imperial splendour, standards high with the feeble sunlight glinting off the battered shields and spears. Marcus Araldites, battle-hardened centurion and veteran of the Sicilian campaign, marched at the head of the column, his eyes, as he sang, relentlessly searching through the mist for signs of rebellious Gauls. These itinerant fighters frequently skirmished with the Roman troops, appearing as if from nowhere to cut the throat of any hapless legionnaire who stopped to do up a sandal or answer a call of nature, then disappearing just as mysteriously into the inhospitable landscape.

The IVth had been in Gaul for three long years, at first fighting in the vanguard of Caesar's all-conquering army but now battling the insurgency led by the wily Vercingetorix, Gaulish freedom fighter and long-haired dude. The current troubles had begun in Orleans, where Roman merchants sub-contracting for lucrative reconstruction business had been slaughtered by the rebels. Julius Caesar himself had returned from Britain to take command and bring the territory back under the heel of Rome. Not that Caesar had any regrets about leaving the damp island outpost of empire; the weather was dreadful and there were no decent dentists.

Araldites glanced up at the sun. The morning was all but spent and he wanted to make the garrison town of Betamax before nightfall. The road was in good repair—and why not, he thought with pride; it was the IVth who had built much of it, certainly the kerbside guttering. With a weatherproof camber and pulverized bedrock, it powered straight as a ruler through the countryside, although even he would admit the services dotted along its length were pretty ordinary, with food you'd think twice about giving to a dog and toilets even the dog wouldn't think about using. And on a public holiday the traffic banked back all the way to Delphinium. Still, it was a world's best-practice example of Roman can-do and for Araldites it simply proved the empire's superiority over the backward, garlic-loving Gauls with their smelly cheeses and bad attitude.

All around them, the land lay in smouldering, blackened ruin. Vercingetorix was running a scorched-earth policy to starve the invading Romans out but with typical Gallic recalcitrance the peasant farmers burned everything except their crops, not wanting to risk losing the generous agricultural subsidies. The cohorts simply helped themselves to corn, fruit or gourmet olives, and the tavernas and trattorias plied their trade in the fortified towns with little interruption. But a recent order from Caesar's tribunes now insisted that money be paid; the hearts and minds of the locals were to be won over even if the rebels were to be disembowelled.

Araldites could see in the near distance a road side stall offering mandarins at four sestertii a tray with an honesty bowl for payment, the farmers being far too afraid to show their faces and collect the money. The legionnaires marched past it without a sideways glance; Araldites' men were not big fruit-eaters. Meat-lover's pizza plus a side of boar ribs was more their style, with plenty of sweet Italian wine to wash it down—none of this Bordeaux crap. Special supplies were shipped in from Rome to make the soldiers feel at home, along with harlots from the Aventine and lyre players to accompany the latest odes set to music.

Deep in the ranks, two legionnaires were discussing that very thing as they trudged along.

'It's not the lyre, it's the lyric that's important,' argued Julius Marlowe, a fresh young recruit from Pompeii in his first year of military service.

'I hears you, bro,' but you are way out o' line—you ain't got the lyre, you ain't got shit,' retorted his friend Snoopius Canis, trying to give his marching as much strut as he could. 'You got a poem, tha's what you got. And poems is for pussies.'

'Then you ain't never read Catullus, man,' said Julius, desperately translating what he remembered of his tutor's words into an argot that could be understood by a cohort grunt. 'He is way gay, that bro' writin' heavy shit.'

Julius had found it difficult settling into army life; the sight of blood made him feel positively nauseous and he kept his philosophical objection to Caesar's imperial ambitions a secret. It was his father who had insisted on enlistment and Julius meekly agreed, harbouring as he did a private ambition to meet babes. So far the only women he'd encountered in Gaul had more hair than a flock of mountain goats and were far less amenable.

Marching on the other side, the portly Caius Lexus, with his usual canny knack of bringing the mood down, entered the debate. 'I know he's commercial but you can't go past Plautus for pure entertainment. Still, let's face it,' he added, frowning. 'When are we ever going to be back in Rome for a festival?' And with that cheery thought they fell silent, hitched their backpacks higher and resignedly planted one foot in front of the other as they had done for so many leagues.

Far above them in the wooded screes, eyes were watching. Asterix and Genuflex the Gauls lay in hiding, surveying the Roman column as it made its way to the relative safety of the earthen ramparts and wooden palisades of Betamax. When the soldiers had passed from view, Asterix signalled his partner to crawl away with him in retreat over the brow of the hill.

'Not much we can do now, *mon ami*. The Roman pigs will keep for another day. Shall we do lunch?'

'But we only have three hours!' cried Genuflex in horror.

'Ah well,' shrugged Asterix, 'we'll have to squeeze it in somehow. No sacrifice is too great *pour la guerre*. I have a gourd of burgundy—I think you shall find its insouciance amusing.'

Genuflex gave a grunt of approval and they withdrew through the still-smouldering meadow to a nearby café offering *moules et boules* and a reasonably priced *menu touristique*.

The cohort reached Betamax as the sun fell behind the hills, and once the great wooden gates had shut firmly behind them, the men scattered to their dormitories to freshen up and slip into something more comfortable. Araldites reported to the regional commander in the praetorium behind the field-temple of Minerva. He found his superior reading a scroll newly arrived from Rome, anxiety furrowing his already weatherbeaten brow. With a heavy sigh, Octavius Jenkins (his mother hailed from Londinium) threw the scroll onto the table and turned to his junior officer.

'Honestly, Araldites, sometimes I think Gaul can go to Hades! And you know as well as I do that if it wasn't for the lavender oil we wouldn't be here at all, that's what this whole war is about: Rome just can't get enough lavender oil. Want to hear the latest from home? According to our masters, the insurgency is under control. Hello? That particular piece of good news is just a tad late for the 6 000 soldiers massacred by Ambiorix—that was a legion and a half, for Jupiter's sake! Most of the country's nothing but ashes, the people loathe us and the drain on the treasury is uncountable. Plus the aquaduct's blocked and we still haven't received the holiday pay—how am I going to break that to the men?'

Araldites remained silent. He avoided political intrigue and simply stayed loyal to Caesar. His brother-in-law had served under Crassus in Mesopotamia, following his master to an identical fate: beheading by the Parthians and no long-service leave. With the untimely death of Crassus, the ruling triumvirate had been cut down to an uneasy duet between Pompey and Caesar—two-party politics and you had no choice but to throw your lot in with either. Funny way to run an empire, he thought.

'And we're being sent a new governor,' continued Octavius. 'Senator Minimus' cousin Cloddus, who despite having a wall-eye and fewer brains than a Goth, has been deemed the best man for the job. I'm sure it helps to come from a family with a majority stake in the providores that feed the legion and a controlling interest in the foundry that forges 80 per cent of our swords—obviously being one lantern short of a dim light is no obstacle to advancement either! He arrives next ides and wants a coin minted to celebrate the occasion. Personally, I can think of a far more constructive use for a disc of red-hot metal when he gets here but I suspect it would mean the end of my career. Anyway, what news of your patrol?'

'No problems, sir,' answered Araldites. 'The gooks—sorry, the Gauls—stayed hidden. We heard rumours of activity outside the red zone and a rebel retreat but it's kinda hard to read the situation on the ground. And I think the men could do with a little down time, a little R and R.'

'Couldn't we all? Alright, tavern leave for all ranks tonight and throw an extra pig on the spit. And make it a double happy hour in the brothels. Now if you'll excuse me, Captain, I've got a meeting with a delegation of local tribal chiefs who want to pledge allegiance to Rome in exchange for free trade with the empire. Tell me when we're having fun, won't you?'

———

In the less salubrious district of Betamax, far from the temples, Claudio's Taverna sat amidst the hovels and garbage pits. Feeble oil lamps barely illuminated the yellow ribbons and tattered banner that read 'Keeping the Fight in Our Boys!' above the door. True to its sentiment, a drunken soldier came crashing through the wattles, propelled by a judiciously placed boot. Inside, Julius and Snoopius sat in a dingy corner nursing their wine goblets as a comic actor on a morale-boosting tour from Rome worked through his material on a tiny stage.

'So this centurion walks into a bar, he holds up two fingers, spreads 'em apart and says to the barman, "I'll have five beers thanks. And a martinus." And the barman says, "Don't you mean martini?" And the soldier says, "No, I only want the one." Then the barman looks at the long-haired peasant with him and says "You've got a gall coming in here." Eh? Gaul? I tell you what though, I was born unlucky. I was named after the god Janus but my first name's Hugh. Hugh Janus. Hey, c'mon, people, work with me here …'

Snoopius sniffed dismissively. 'I seen a dog wi' no legs doin' a better stand-up than that. Let's get us some ho's and get outta here.'

Julius choked on his Lambrusco. Claudio's girls were widely known to carry at least six communicable diseases and that was when they were still dressed. 'I think I'll wait for the band,' he said lamely. 'Rumour has it, Snoopius …'

'Say wha,?'

'Er … I been hearin' some shit, says we're goin' to lay siege to the rebels in Alesia.'

'Where the Hade' that?'

'Issa town in the hills. Caesar pushin' 'em in there for a last stand kinda thing,' said Julius, struggling to reduce military strategy to words of one syllable.

'Yeah, and yo know why the bitch doin' dat? He fightin' Pompey, man, not the Gauls! This place don't count fo' shit, 'xcept for their lavender oil. Hey, I don' even use dat stuff but here I am puttin' my sorry ass on the line so some fancy senator can keep his butt smellin' fresh! And my main man Caesar, he want the glory—you hear wha' I'm sayin'? So's he can sass it back to Rome, do the business on Pompey and make hisself emperor! Dat's what this war's all about, Marlowe man, yo take it from Snoopius.'

Julius sat there stunned that his friend had a far better grasp on the political situation than he did. So much for private schools, he thought bitterly. 'But we're bringing civilisation to these people …' he stammered, jivus talk going completely out of his head.

Snoopius raised an eyebrow, looking around him as two inebriated centurions held the barkeeper's head in a slop bucket, egged on by their comrades and the casual staff. 'Yo call this civilisation?' he said incredulously. 'So some chief puts on a toga and builds hisself a villa, calls hisself a friend o' Rome—hey, why not? We done killed ev'rybody else and an'body left standin' ain't got a pot to piss in! What else they gonna do? I dunno what dictionary you is lookin' in, my friend, but that ain't the meanin' o' civilisation in my book.'

Julius studied his goblet in confusion as on the other side of the room, two figures hugged the shadows and observed proceedings. With their long, give away Gallic locks tucked neatly under nondescript berets, Asterix and Genuflex had quietly scaled the perimeter walls to take advantage of the half-price *pastis* being offered at Claudio's. Any scraps of information they could glean and still remember in the morning would be invaluable to the resistance and they might even be able to reimburse themselves for the night from petty cash. Feeling a little peckish, Genuflex put his hands into his pocket and took out a small cloth bundle as he reached for a crust of bread. An unmistakeable, acrid odour of wet wool and un-washed sandals rose from the block of cheese the moment he unwrapped it. He looked at Asterix in alarm.

Araldites, newly arrived at the bar for a mug of honeyed wine, sniffed the air. 'Gauls!' he yelled and leapt across the room, tackling the hapless rebels to the ground as legionnaires piled on from all sides. Under cover of the arrest, they trashed the gaming tables and broke the barkeeper's arm for good measure. Half an hour later, the two prisoners were led, trussed and gagged, before the commander.

'This had better be good, Araldites,' said Octavius as he entered the praetorium. 'We were just about to start on the complimentary buffet.'

'Two Gallic spies, sir. Caught in the compound red-handed—and they didn't pick up their bar tab.'

'Aha!' said Octavius as he regarded the two wretches. 'Well, what do you know? What have we here? Asterix, able lieutenant of the mighty Vercingetorix, no less. This is quite a coup. But I don't know the other one …'

'I'm Genuflex, sir. I've never met this man before in my life, I swear, I don't know anything about the make-or-break plan to rout the legion at …'

'Shut up you idiot!' hissed Asterix. '*Pas devant les soldats!*'

'No, go right ahead, you may speak before us,' said Octavius, chuckling. 'I'm afraid I understand the lingo, Asterix—I was an exchange student before I joined the army.'

Asterix and Genuflex fell silent.

'So, you won't talk? Perhaps a little gentle persuasion will help you change your minds. Guards, strip them and force them to make a naked human pyramid!'

'A pyramid of two?' asked Araldites doubtfully.

'Alright, a column and plinth, whatever! But the humiliation will break their spirits.'

'*Donnez-moi liberté ou mort!*' spat Asterix, straining against his bonds.

'No, I'm sorry, my lingo isn't that good. Missed that entirely,' apologised Octavius.

'Give me liberty or death!' said Asterix slowly in Latin.

'I wouldn't have thought the two were mutually exclusive, in a spiritual sense,' said Octavius, enjoying himself as he toyed with his prisoners' minds. 'Come on, you Gallic scum, spill the beans—we know where your families live.'

'I have no family, sir,' stammered Genuflex. 'I didn't think it was a responsible decision to start one, what with all the travelling a rebel has to do …'

'Will you be quiet!' screamed Asterix. 'You are giving completely the wrong impression of *la gloire de Gaul*! Be a man! *Resistance!*'

'Well, that's self-explanatory,' said Octavius, turning to Araldites. 'Same word, same meaning, just a different pronunciation. But I tire of these games. Guards! Prepare the thumbscrews, the burning pitch, the hot irons and tell that comic actor he's doing a forty-minute set in the torture room.'

'No!' cried Genuflex, 'anything but that!'

Asterix shrugged off the legionnaires pulling him roughly to his feet and stood to his full height. He glared at Octavius, spat on the ground and defiantly shouted '*Vive la Gaul!*'

Suddenly the door burst open and Lexus, red-faced and panting, staggered into the room. 'Sir, a messenger has arrived from Caesar— the Germanic tribes have crossed the Rhine and are bearing down upon us!'

Asterix and Genuflex looked at each other and shrieked. Throwing himself on the floor before Octavius, Asterix blubbered, 'A thousand pardons, *monsieur le Commandant*! I surrender completely, I'll tell you everything I know, but by all the gods in Rome I beg of you—save us from the Germans!'

AD 0.02

A saviour doesn't sleep through

The wail of a disgruntled infant shattered what had been a relatively silent, nay, holy night in Bethlehem. The sudden disturbance set to barking the mangy curs slinking through the shadows, and two stables down a donkey brayed disconsolately. In the lowly cowshed Joseph had just nodded off, despite the discomfort of lying on a pallet with the odd thistle poking into his back. Waking with a start, he searched about through the straw for his sandals and muttered darkly to himself.

'Jesus Christ!'

'That's not a bad name,' said Mary, lying awake beside him. 'I like it better than Warren. But I don't know that your mother'll be too thrilled.'

'Jesus it will be. Mother be damned; it's not like she's come good on the offers to babysit,' said Joseph, picking up the mewling infant and delivering him to Mary's breast with a little more vigour than was strictly necessary. 'How long till he leaves home?'

Mary sighed. She couldn't blame Joseph for feeling underwhelmed by the whole experience. She suspected that he hadn't been entirely convinced by the news of the archangel visiting her all those months ago—he'd spent three days in the shed sharpening his chisels after she told him. And the baby's arrival had been nothing like that promised by the prenatal classes; her birth plan had gone right out the window at the first contraction and Joseph's feeble back-rubs had proved all but useless. And before that he'd had to walk beside the donkey through that long and desperate journey, then endure the awful mix-up with the accommodation because they wouldn't accept Armenian Express, and now, to top it all off, he had to sleep in a cowshed even though the poor man was lactose-intolerant.

A sudden noise made her glance outside. 'Joseph,' she hissed, pulling at his sleeve, 'there's a man going through the garbage bins!'

'He's probably the chef from that bloody awful hotel restaurant preparing the breakfasts. The only thing round here that gets recycled.'

As they watched, the figure quietly replaced the bin lid, dusted off his hands and, with a furtive look around, made for their door. Joseph stood ready in the shadows, armed with a malodorous nappy. There was a knock, then a dapper little man wearing Calvary Klein robes came through the door with a cocky swagger.

'Saw your star on, thought I'd drop in,' he said, proffering a business tablet. 'Harrius M the Miller.'

'What does the M stand for?' asked Mary suspiciously.

'A thousand. My mother was into numerology. You're probably wondering what I'm doing here at this time of the morning.'

'I take it you're not selling encyclopaedias,' said Joseph.

'Nice one, squire,' said Harrius with a sly grin. 'Hasn't been anyone else sniffing around here, has there?'

'If it was any business of yours, we'd tell you,' said Joseph angrily.

'Keep your hair shirt on, Gramps.'

Joseph bristled. He was sensitive about his age. He was practically old enough to be his wife's grandfather and he'd seen the raised eyebrows and knowing winks when Mary's belly had swollen to the point where nobody was buying the wind-retention story.

'Peace, Joseph,' said Mary. 'Three shepherds were here earlier, bearing gifts, which was very nice of them, although I don't know what we're going to do with five litres of sheep dip and a crutching tool. Oh, and a real estate agent arrived wanting to know if we were looking for a bigger place now we'd started a family.'

'Don't miss a trick, do they? Might be able to take the sheep dip off your hands, I know this bloke, owes me a favour. The reason I ask is I hear you've got the Son of God on the premises,' said Harrius, looking around intently for a manger.

Joseph let out a strangulated laugh. 'He's either that or the son of the Abyssinian exchange student who just happened to be staying with …'

'Don't be ridiculous, Joseph,' Mary cut in. 'But, sir, what does a miller want with my boy? Do you bring gifts of flour?'

'No, I gave away the milling business years ago, not enough bread in it—you with me? But it cost a fortune to have those business tablets carved, so I'm stuck with the name. I've had a lot of fingers in a lot of pies. Import, export, flogging antiques to the Romans. Nowadays, I'm into celebrity management …'

'What is a celebrity?'

'That's kind of hard to explain. It's a famous person who doesn't really do anything.'

'Then what are they famous for?' asked Joseph, puzzled.

'For being famous, of course. You know, they hang around with the right crowd, always at the Temple on the big feast days, get their graven images into the right places.'

'And what is management?'

'Ah, even more of a mystery, that one. I'm not exactly sure myself—but it's a growth industry, I can tell you that much. Basically, people pay me to pay the celebrities to turn up and …'

'Do nothing?' ventured Mary.

'There you go, you're getting the hang of it—you could have a career in the personality industry if the Mother of the Son of God thing falls flat. But I don't just do celebrities. I do media consultancy …'

'What is media?'

'Now, why did I think you'd ask that? It's the latest thing from Rome. Fantastic. You know they've even got a talkback oracle there now? The soothsayer, he stands at one end of the Forum yelling through a bull horn and citizens can shout questions at him through a lead pipe from the other. And whatever the oracle says, that's what the people believe. Very popular. Even Caesar's down there every morning paying homage, taking a few calls. Then there's your more traditional hand-scribed scrolls—would you believe the *Sinai Morning Herald* circulation has gone up to 38? Incredible!'

'But what has all this to do with us?'

'Well, I can generate a lot of media interest in your boy if I play my cards right. Sure, prophets are ten a shekel—just last week I did lunch with Joshua the Seer—you heard of him? Reckons he's the illegitimate twin brother of the King of the Israelites. Like, one twin is legitimate and the other one's not? Please. So I said, "Josh, you prove it, I'll move it." I tell you, Mary—mind if I call you Mary?'

'I'm Joseph.'

'My mistake. I tell you, Joe, even if they looked like second cousins I could have him on *LX Minutes* this Sunday.'

Joseph and Mary looked at each other blankly as Harrius paused for breath. 'But, Mr M,' stammered Mary, 'our child is truly the Son of God.'

'Sure, sure. Any distinguishing features to verify the claim? Has he got "If lost return to God" written on his backside?'

'He has a halo,' said Mary, deeply offended yet wholly unaware that she was beginning a long and hallowed tradition of Christian umbrage.

'No good. Haloes don't reproduce on papyrus. We could mock something up but your average punter isn't an idiot. What am I saying? He's a complete drongo! But that's a trade secret, pretend I never said it. Nah, what we need is an angle, something's that going to make Mr and Mrs Western Jerusalem, sitting in the apothecary's waiting room, want to pick up a scroll with your boy on the cover. A burning bush, the face of Moses in the tea-leaves, stuff like that. Has he done any miracles? People love a miracle.'

'He passed water into wine earlier this morning.'

'Yes,' said Joseph bitterly, 'just before I drank it! Mind you, he couldn't make it taste any worse.'

'No offence, J of A, but I think we need a bit more chutzpah. No stools in the shape of the patriarchs? Interesting family members—but please, none of that Nebuchar begat Bebuchar, got to keep it simple for the tabloids. How about Mum and Dad, any saucy secrets from the bedchamber?'

Mary blushed deeply. 'Sir, I am a virgin!'

'So the kid's got to be adopted, right? Hmm … might be something in that, especially if Daddy's a Roman governor or a priest of the Temple Mount, your quality journals can't get enough of that kind of story.'

'He is born of me, sir, but his conception was platonic,' murmured Mary modestly.

Joseph harrumphed behind the byre. Harrius raised his eyebrows. 'Platonic? How does that work? I know my ex-wife only had to think about having a baby and hey, another child support payment I've got to figure out how to avoid, but you don't look the type.'

'God sent the archangel Gabriel to whisper in my ear.'

'Really? You're sure he didn't whisper someplace else?' Mary shook her head modestly. 'In your ear, huh? Well, that's something you don't see every day. I think we can call that an angle. Is this Gabriel around, maybe I could get a few quotes.'

'Haven't seen him since,' said Joseph darkly.

'Doesn't matter, would've been a plus, that's all. Okay, I think we can hammer out a deal.'

There was a knock at the door. 'We're expecting Three Wise Men,' said Joseph.

'In this town? You're kidding me! 'said Harrius, taking a look out the window. 'Nah, it's the delivery boy. This contract's going to take all night so I ordered a takeaway. Loaves and fishes okay with you guys?'

AD 37

The first Christmas
after the first one

The door of Mortecai's tavern creaked open and a stiff breeze off the Sea of Galilee sent the oil lamps guttering. Japheth the shepherd nervously poked his head into the smoky room, vainly scanning the shadowy alcoves for the friends he was due to meet. Typical, he thought: always the first to arrive. From across the room a fisherman complained bitterly about the draught so Japheth quickly shut the door and edged his way towards the bar, sniffing surreptitiously at his tunic. He sighed. No matter how many times he washed it and thrashed it on the rocks, he couldn't get rid of the smell of frightened sheep; for such a stupid animal they had a highly developed sense of the melodramatic. No wonder he didn't have a girlfriend. Being forty-two and having a walleye wasn't a great help either but still, Japheth was convinced a grease-free set of threads could change his life.

'What'll it be?' asked Mortecai.

'Honeyed wine,' said Japheth, fumbling through his satchel for a few shekels.

'Good choice,' said Mortecai, 'seeing it's all we've got. Drinking alone?'

It's the tunic, thought Japheth, always the tunic. 'No,' he stammered, 'I'm meeting some old friends, we're having a bit of a reunion tonight.'

'School do, is it? Graduating year of 5 BC, that sort of thing?'

Japheth didn't even know what a school was. 'No. We, um, we met many years ago in Bethlehem. In a stable.'

Mortecai's eyes narrowed. 'Must have been some night.'

'It changed my life,' said Japheth awkwardly. To his relief, a flurry of wind announced new arrivals and he turned to see his old friend Matthew the shepherd framed in the doorway.

'Matthew! Over here!' called Japheth.

'Mine's a honeyed wine, you old bastard!' cried Matthew, who was slightly hard of hearing and automatically assumed everyone else was as well. He eased himself onto a gopherwood bar stool and gestured to the man who'd walked in alongside him. 'You remember this geezer, don't you?'

'Of course,' said Japheth. Isaac, the third shepherd. He hadn't seen him in ages.

'Thirty-four years, eh? Who'd've thought?' said Isaac. 'Just a juice for me thanks, barkeep—I'm designated cart driver for tonight and I noticed the roads are full of Nazareth's finest, being the holiday weekend and all. Can't afford a ticket, not a man of my position.'

There was an awkward silence. 'So, Isaac,' said Japheth, never much good at small talk despite hours of practice with his flock, 'still into sheep?'

'Those charges were never proved—no, it's alright Matthew, I'm quite happy to talk about it—but frankly, Japheth, the whole episode left such a bitter taste in my mouth I moved into goats. I've got two shops now in Jerusalem, just outside the Temple gate.'

'The Temple?' asked Japheth, suddenly interested.

'Too right. I even supply the Romans for feast days,' said Isaac, with the smug pride of the successful businessman.

'You must have seen Jesus attack the moneylenders.'

Isaac frowned. 'Hmm, yes, bit of an embarrassment, that. Not quite the best way to go about things in my book. I mean, if you *have* got a legitimate grievance, there are proper channels...'

'But surely as King of the Jews ...'

'Aha!' said Isaac, waving an admonitory finger, 'self-proclaimed King of the Jews. Very different story. Let's get our facts right, as the high priest said to the ...'

'But you witnessed our Lord's nativity!'

'I've witnessed an awful lot of things, Japheth. And I was very young at the time. Let's face it, we were all overexcited, what with the star and the census forms and what have you ...'

'But surely there was no mistaking the divine radiance of Mary?' urged the bewildered Japheth.

'She was a very nice lady, absolutely, under the circumstances ...'

'What do you mean, circumstances?'

'Well, did you see a ring on her finger?' asked Isaac with raised eyebrows.

Japheth bristled. Matthew cleared his throat noisily. 'Allright lads, calm down—what say we keep the reminiscences till the others get here, eh?'

Isaac looked pointedly into his olive juice. 'Did you manage to get hold of the little drummer boy? Parupapumpum?' asked Japheth sullenly.

'Well, I couldn't find anyone under that name in the tax records. Either he hasn't filed an activity statement for a few years or he's died. Hey—funny thing though. Have you had a visit from any of the disciples?'

Japheth and Isaac shook their heads.

'I had Mark round my place the other day, all very businesslike with the stylus and the wax tablet, asking for my account of that first Christmas; who was there, who gave what, that sort of stuff.'

'Maybe he's writing a book,' ventured Isaac.

'Could be. Anyway, I said to be perfectly honest, I only offered a lamb because I thought there might be a barbecue on—I even had some unleavened garlic bread in my saddle bag but it didn't seem the right time to bring it out.'

As Matthew paused for air, there was a frail voice behind him. 'We have ridden long and seek the shepherd Matthew.' He turned and there stood three venerable ancients, clothed in musty silks, bent almost double under the weight of their magnificent jewels which glistered and baubled in the flickering light.

'Hey, wise guys! Long time no seek!' cried Matthew, slapping Balthasar heartily on the back, shaking hands all round. 'Here, have a seat.'

'Thanks, but I think we'll stand,' said Caspar. 'We've been stuck on those camels all day. Eight hours just from Capernaum, the traffic's murder.'

'Oy, am I getting too old for this or what?' added Melchior. 'That's the last time I leave the Orient.'

'Do you do valet stabling?' Balthasar asked Mortecai. 'There's three camels outside need a drink and there's three wee kings right here hanging out for a stiff one as well.'

'On the tab, Mortecai,' said Matthew. 'So how have you been, fellas? Keeping busy?'

'Pretty quiet. Not much call for wise men these days. We pay homage to the odd prophet, consult the heavens, same old stuff,' said Balthasar. 'I was sorry to hear about Jesus.'

'Yeah, not good,' muttered Matthew, as a reflective silence fell. 'You don't mess with the Romans.'

'I read a poll in the *Jerusalem Herald*,' said Isaac. 'Eighty per cent said the Romans did the right thing crucifying him. Eighty per cent.'

'When we stood in that stable all those years ago, I never thought it'd come to that,' sighed Caspar. 'Mind you, I wasn't expecting miracles but I kept thinking maybe he is the one … I mean, there has to be something better out there somewhere. But now—who knows?'

'He lives, Caspar. The Son of God lives.'

'Oh, really, Japheth? He looked pretty dead to me,' said Isaac.

'You have no faith!'

'Ah, faith,' mused Balthasar. 'The substance of things hoped for, quicksilver of the yearning soul.'

'Absolutely,' said Matthew, not having a clue what Balthasar was on about. 'Look, I don't know if Jesus was the chosen one or not. The way I see it, he was a decent bloke who did a lot for the local fishing industry. Bloody good public speaker as well. Why they had to crucify him is beyond me.'

'A prophet is not without honour, save in his own country, and in his own house,' pronounced Melchior.

'I must remember that for her indoors,' said Matthew with a laugh, trying to get the evening going. 'Same again, lads?'

They all nodded agreement. 'Balthasar,' said Japheth intently, 'you journeyed hundreds of miles, you brought gifts—why go to all that effort if you didn't truly think the Messiah had been born?'

'Look, in our business you have to play the percentages. Is there one true faith or two? How about three? Look at how many gods the Romans worship. And out east, past where we come from, they follow this guy called Buddha who says there isn't a god at all!'

'Maybe,' said Melchior, 'but I still think if God did not exist, it would be necessary for man to invent him.'

'Melchior, you gotta write some of this stuff down, it's gold,' said Balthasar. 'Anyway, Japheth, there's an awful lot of prophets out there and frankly, I for one don't know which of them is handing out the valid passports to paradise.'

'So, of all of us am I the only believer in Jesus?' asked Japheth incredulously.

'Would it make a difference if you were?' said Caspar gently.

'Well, no,' stammered Japheth, confused.

'Hey, I believe in the man—we've had him round for dinner,' said Matthew. 'And boy, could he make food stretch!'

'He always had a kind word for the little people,' conceded Isaac, 'but he knew nothing about small business. You've got to look out for number one. People make choices and if they decide not to improve their lot in life …'

'Hardly a Christian attitude,' chided Melchior.

'Did you just make that up? The Christian word? Follower of Christ—I like it!' said Balthasar admiringly. 'Still, can't see it catching on. All very well having a message but these days you gotta have messengers.'

'We will carry forth the message, Balthasar,' said Japheth warmly. 'And one day the peoples of the world will live a life of quiet dignity, tolerance and charity.'

'Maybe,' said Melchior with a shrug.

'I'm sorry, Melchior, but I have to say this. The way you do that shrug, that "I know something that you don't" shrug, it really pisses me off,' fumed Japheth.

'I'm a wise man, Japheth, cynicism is part of the job description,' said Melchior mildly. 'You have found your saviour and for you I am happy—I envy you your certainty, I really do. However, others will travel very different paths— some will not feel the need to even venture forth. But mark my words: all will steel themselves in the moral rectitude of their own convictions, to the world's lasting misery.'

There was a silence as Melchior finished and drained his goblet. Caspar eventually spoke. 'Your words depress me, Melchior.'

'Oh, it's something I read on a scroll when I was wating for a doctor in Athens. Made a lot of sense,' said Melchior.

Matthew could feel the reunion sliding rapidly towards a dud night out. He reached into his satchel and pulled out some packages. 'Hey, I brought gifts!'

There were oohs and aahs of admiration as the offerings were opened and admired. 'Socks and a camel grooming kit, fantastic!' cried Balthasar.

'"Rules" of this Shoppe,' read Isaac as he unrolled his novelty papyrus. 'Matthew, you shouldn't have.'

'Well, it's how we started out and I just thought we should make it a tradition. Once a year we'll get together, remember Jesus and exchange gifts in memory of a great guy.'

'The Son of God,' corrected Japheth.

'Whatever,' said Matthew, busily folding the discarded wrapping cloths for next time.

'I could be pushing up saltbush this time next year,' said Blathasar gloomily.

'Well, your kids can take over, make it a family affair.'

'Oh, great,' said Isaac.

'Caspar and I decided against children long ago,' said Melchior. 'It's a lifestyle choice.'

'And I respect that,' said Matthew, somewhat nervously. 'What did Jesus say—judge not lest ye yourself be judged?'

'Indeed he did, my friend,' said Balthasar. 'Let's drink to that.'

'Sorry, gentlemen,' said Mortecai as they went to charge their goblets. 'The bar tab's run out. It'll cost you plus the surcharge for public holidays.'

'Well, Matthew,' said Balthasar, reaching for his purse,

'looks like the spirit of Christmas is well and truly established. Gentlemen, for what it's worth, in the name of our late lamented friend I give you peace, joy and goodwill to all men on earth.'

They raised their goblets and solemnly drank.

'Amen to that,' said Matthew. 'Now: who's for the buffet?'

No time
in particular

A short history
of the stage

Theatre began in ancient Greece with the first performance of *The Mousetrap*, by Agathos Christos.
A searing indictment of Athenian butlers, it opened
at the Theatre of Dionysius in 414 BC and has run continu-
ously ever since, except for a brief interruption when the
Romans inadvertently wiped out the second touring cast in
Gaul. The play's success (and the royalties it generated)
inspired tragedians such as Sophocles and Aeschylus to drama-
tise Greek myths and legends, allowing audiences to enjoy
such hits as *Greece—the Musical!* and *Olive!* Aristophanes,
with his off beat comedy *Frogs Out of Work*, was universally
condemned by the intelligentsia yet enjoyed great success at
the box office, a term derived from the ancient Greek word
boxos, meaning credit card handling fee.

Children's theatre also had its beginnings in the classical
world. Hard on the heels of the invention of schools came the
invention of school holidays and harried Greek mothers could
unload their bored offspring for an hour or four to watch *Noddy
in Troyland* or *Dolmade the Dinosaur*, a show featuring four

rural simpletons dressed in brightly coloured tunics dancing with someone on work experience wearing a character suit. In a curious twist of fate, these entertainers became the wealthiest people in the land, a fact that has baffled archaeologists for centuries.

As the power of Athens waned and the Romans waxed (ostensibly for a better look in sandals), theatre became the most popular form of entertainment after gladiatorial combat and X box, a deceptively simple game revolving around placing ten items in a box. Occasionally the drama and violent spectacle were combined, as in AD 46, when the first amateur cast of *Godspell*, a musical drawn from the emerging Christianity, was fed to the lions under the orders of Claudius, who had seen a matinee and didn't think much of it. More to imperial liking were the works of Plautus and Terence, who also wrote less formal *buffo* pieces under the name of Terry. However, the fall of Rome and the spread of the Barbarians was bad news for a theatre industry already struggling with the effects of late-night shopping and the Gothic predilection for sport of any kind; the theatres closed and the lights went out on the Appian Way.

In the East, theatre emerged from the folktale traditions. Bedouins were early masters of the tent show, endlessly travelling the deserts of Arabia to pitch their tents and give light comedies like *Caravan* and *The Road to Morocco*. In India, a hive of theatrical industry grew around the ancient port city of Mumbai and busy actors could find themselves performing in ten plays at once, running from stage to stage desperately trying to remember which character they were playing next. The Mahabharata, adapted from the world's longest narrative poem, was confusing at the best of times but became all but impenetrable when performed by a cast that changed every fifteen minutes. In China, the dissonant atonalism of the nascent Peking Opera gave opera a reputation that it has fought to throw off ever since: oblique, incomprehensible and interminable. Far more pleasing to the crowds were the martial arts action plays that toured the provinces on the back of an ox-cart. These slapstick performers often became local heroes, telling simple tales of good and evil through a mixture of face-pulling, yelling and arse-numbingly painful bone fracturing.

It wasn't until the Middle Ages that Western theatre as we know it today (live performance, preferably with some sort of government subsidy) re-emerged in fairgrounds and religious festivals. 'Mumming', the enacting of morality tales by itinerant players, reached its peak when theatrical super troupe The Mummers and the Paupers toured *Everyman and his Dog* through the plague hot spots of Europe in the fifteenth century—a production that still holds the record for the number of understudies required. Despite the risk, actors were prepared to chance a painful death because the job beat waiting tables and there was every chance they might pick up an agent.

Farce also emerged at this time in France and Italy, where farce-bandits grouped together to form *comedia dell'arte* troupes, performing low comedies to rowdy tavern audiences. Plots were predictable—wife goes away, saucy wench is employed by hapless master, wife returns with hilarious results—but theatre goers couldn't get enough of them, especially on nights when the beer was offered half-price. Civic authorities, fearing public disquiet and moral recklessness, banned the practice of farce-ing until the tireless anti-censorship campaigner Countess Margaret of Pomeranz successfully petitioned the Pope to allow it to continue, thus ensuring a tradition that has evolved triumphantly into the theatre-restaurant of the modern era.

The Elizabethans saw a flourishing of the English drama. In 1576, James Burbage built the first permanent theatre in England, known, somewhat unimaginatively, as The Theatre.

Competitors followed, and soon Londoners could watch plays in The Other Theatre or The Completely Different Theatre. William Shakespeare broke with tradition and called his playhouse The Globe. Built on the south bank of the Thames, it is described famously in the prologue to his play *Henry V* as 'this wooden O'. The original plan had been to build a 'wooden B' but the acoustics were terrible and half the audience couldn't see the stage. Council rejected plans for a 'wooden D' but compromise was finally reached and the world's most famous theatre opened for business in 1598 with a Morning Melodies session for senior citizens.

Despite this early planning authority setback, Shakespeare still ranks as the greatest playwright in the English language. Son of a glove-maker from Stratford, he journeyed to London as a young man with his heart set on becoming an actress, an occupation which he discovered to be illegal at the time. So he became an actor instead and because no-one was giving him any good parts, eventually began to write his own plays, filled with enormous roles that had him centre stage for as long as possible. A gifted poet and brilliant linguist, Shakespeare actually invented many words we use in the English language today, such as 'assassination', 'bump' and 'radar'. He is also responsible for more schools matinees than any other playwright, although some of his plays have been attributed to Christopher Marlowe, scholars believing that a poorly educated man like Shakespeare would be incapable of such poetic flights of genius. An unfair accusation—think of our own time, when literary giants such as Snoop Doggy Dog barely made it through grade school.

Under Cromwell and the Puritans, funding for theatre dried up, because the words 'a good night out' did not appear in the Bible. So actors went back to their real jobs and wrote desultory grant applications on the off-chance. Things looked up when the monarchy was reinstated—queens have always played a big role in show business—and the Restoration comedies of Wycherly and Congreve gave audiences just what they longed for: three hours sleep. Women were now finally permitted to act upon the public stage and immediately began to complain that there weren't enough decent parts for them, particularly once they'd hit fourty. But despite the novelty of female actors, or actresses as they as wished to be called to subvert the patriarchal tyranny of lexicography, audience numbers dropped off. Crime was enjoying a revival of popularity, being relatively straightforward and affordable, and it wasn't until the eighteenth century, when characters stopped saying 'A pox on't!' every five minutes and plots were simplified to the point where they could be understood without a PhD, that the general public once more embraced the stage.

By the nineteenth century, theatre was everywhere; the novelist Charles Dickens went to a live performance every night for two years, each of them different, except for *Les Mis* which he saw eleven times. In the absence of mass media, the theatre was an indispensable part of everyday life for rich and poor alike. As producers vigorously competed against each other, newer, bigger and more fantastical playhouses were built, boasting rich furnishings in red velvet and modern innovations like gas lighting, toilets backstage and signed performances for the deaf. Victorians flocked to the comedies of Oscar Wilde, the operas of Verdi and the dramas of Chekhov; Australians in other states did much the same, except in Queensland, where they preferred community theatre that tackled local issues head-on.

Theatre now roughly divided along social lines. At one end sat the glittering operettas of Offenbach, Strauss and Lehar, the drawing room comedies of the late Victorian age and the intellectual psycho dramas of Ibsen and Strindberg, while at the other sat the populist music hall. Things were ticking along quite nicely until the unimaginable happened in 1914: management stopped the actors' meal allowance on matinee days. Oh, and the First World War broke out. Nothing quite like carnage on the Western Front to put a dent in the attendance figures.

When at last the Armistice was declared and minstrel shows hastily adapted for a male chorus kick-line of one-legged veterans, serious playwrights of the modern era turned a harsh spotlight on the decaying social fabric. Bertolt Brecht, bewildered and confused by the carnage of war, invented a new type of theatre that left his audience equally bewildered and confused. In Weimar Germany, biting satirical cabarets proliferated and did so much to stop the rise of Hitler and the Second World War. Britain turned to the whimsy of Noel Coward and Ivor Novello, hiding from the harsh realities of Depression behind a spangled curtain of make-believe, where everyone was witty and gay, though not necessarily in that order.

War followed the fragile peace as surely as a comic follows an adagio act and when Europe once more dragged herself up from the knees, not even the West End could shut out the real world with greasepaint and an entr'acte ballet. British social realists like John Osborne wrote kitchen-sink dramas questioning contemporary plumbing practices and sexual stereotyping. Joe Orton shocked the staid public with his outrageous comedies, while in America, Arthur Miller dug deep into the national psyche to expose the hypocrisy and injustice of McCarthyism. And let's face it, the tall, dour playwright must have been doing something right—he scored Marilyn Monroe, for God's sake!

But having only just survived the threat presented by

cinema, theatre faced a new challenge: television. In its infancy, the new medium was little more than a stage with cameras pointed at it but as television began to realise its almost limitless potential, theatre could not compete. Home renovation and gardening tips were difficult to stage, an audience with a concentration span of seven minutes hard to hold. So the theatre returned to its core value, that electric point of communication between audience and live performer, reaching its zenith, to many critics' eyes, with Peter Brook's seminal production of *On the Buses—Live!* in 1978.

In Australia, theatre's ability to communicate directly to a local audience was seized upon. Sometimes the audience was localised to seven or eight people but an independent school of theatrical practice grew, telling our stories in our words to our people. Sadly, the industry suffered under our indifference, our apathy and our reluctance to pay full-price for anything, but nonetheless, with a feeble subsidy from the public purse, theatre continues to amaze and delight the hundreds of people who attend.

So whither the stage? In the twenty-first century, can 'we cram within this wooden O the very casques that did affright the air at Agincourt' and piece out its imperfections with our thoughts? Think, when actors 'talk of horses, that we see them printing their proud hoof i' in the receiving earth' and 'turn the accomplishment of many years into an hour-glass'?

Possibly, if there's nudity involved.

AD 989

Danes at sea

The Year of our Lord 989 dawned brightly for Athølred of Danemark. Bidding farewell to his parents one frosty morning in Jånuåry, he left the family farm and ventured off to seek his fame and fortune as an apprentice Viking. When he was knee-high to a grasshøpper, Torstein the Tale-teller had visited their small hamlet, enthralling the villagers with sagas of the long-boats sailed over distant seas by legendary heroes like Eric the Red and his sons Lief and Twïg. Ever since, Athølred had yearned to follow in their watery footsteps. Scarce able to walk, he had tottered about with a small shield and a wooden sword, pillaging the day-care centre and terrorising his tiny playmates. As his muscles firmed and hair sprouted in unusual places he charged about the byre, unleashing blood-curdling yells and (much to their surprise) raping the smaller livestock. Now, broad-shouldered and depilated, he made his way to Trottingholm to join a company of marauders.

On his arrival, the heavy gates of the fortified town lay open for late-night shopping and he walked freely between the earthen dykes, marvelling at the sights and sounds of life in the big city. There must be at least two hundred people here, he realised, head reeling from the scent of pickled ale and mulled fish. Along the wharf, long boats lay moored as their cargoes of sacked treasure, salted cod and underwear were unloaded by short, stocky warriors, while hard-faced women stood by waiting for news of their menfolk still at sea. Dazed, he presented himself at the raiders' compound that lay in the heart of the settlement.

'And what makes you want to be a Viking?' asked the short and stocky man behind the reception desk. He sported a beard as red as holly berries and his one remaining ear was badly scarred.

'I've wished for nothing else,' stammered Athølred.

'You'll have to speak up, I'm a little deaf.'

'Ever since I heard the sagas of the Norsemen …'

'Don't tell me—Torstein the Tale-teller?'

Athølred nodded and let out a bloodcurdling yell to cover his embarrassment.

'We get a lot of his audience members—but you'll find things are very different to the yarns he spins. It takes weeks of training to be a Viking, it's not all rape and pillage, you know. Well, that's a fair bit of it, but you have to know knots as well. Can you do a half-sheepshank? Nah, didn't think so, still wet around the ears, aren't you? But you've got the dream and you're keeping it alive, so we'll take you on. My name's Bjorn and this is Benny,' he said gesturing to a man with hair as white as flax and a bronze earring teamed nicely with a garnet medallion. 'Don't speak any other languages, do you?'

Athølred shook his head.

'Oh well, it helps, but it's not essential. Just handy when we're overseas, you know. Still, they all understand the meaning of this!' he cried, drawing a notched and stubby blade from his belt. Athølred smiled and opened his mouth to yell. 'Best we save the bloodcurdling cries,' Bjorn cut him off. 'Don't want you losing your voice before we hit the beaches.'

He and Benny led Athølred into the inner compound, a muddy yard piled high with stores and weapons, a blacksmith hammering away at his anvil in the corner before a glowing furnace. Ropes were being tarred, sails and nets hung out to dry and masts were being fashioned from spruce trunks by carpenters, the shavings from their adzes filling the air with the sweet resinous perfumes of spruce and trunk. Barracks lined the perimeter and the place teemed with burly men briskly going about their business in a burly yet purposeful manner.

'A bit more purposeful than you expected?' asked Bjorn, seeing Athølred's surprise. 'Like I said, it's not just a couple of lads building a boat and setting sail. No, very professional outfit these days, your Nordic raider. Empire building, that's what we're doing, world's best practice. Right. You can bunk down in E-block. That's E for Elke, they're all named after local girls. Get a good night's sleep because we start training at dawn. Rape practice first thing.'

Athølred's eyes lit up.

'Yeah—downside is, we have to practise on each other. Still, gets you in shape for a long sea voyage. Cultures of the World after that, then an hour of pillaging. Afternoon we do knots—got it?'

The next day at noon, still a little reluctant to sit down after the morning's first lesson, Athølred lined up for his lunch with the other trainees. His mind swirled with interesting facts about Anglo-Saxon culture but already the vocabulary of useful traveller's phrases was going out of his head. All he could remember was 'Could I trouble you to keep still while I dismember you?' He grabbed a platter and took in the vast range of dishes laid out before him.

'Not bad, eh?' said Benny. 'We've just invented it: the

smorgasbord. There's your pickled herring; your herring in aspic; herring in a berry coulis; walnuts; and waffle cones with a choice of two flavours for afters. No fudge sauce today but Bjorn does a nice open sandwich if you're not watching your carbs.'

Taking his food to an upturned barrel, Athølred eased himself down next to yet another short, stocky man, this time with hair as red as blood—actually it was blood, he discovered on closer inspection.

'Not my natural colour,' said the fellow recruit with a grin. 'Fair as wheat, normally. Thorgen's the name—we met this morning, although you probably can't recognise me from this angle. Well, what brings you here?'

'Childhood dream, always wanted to be a Viking.'

'And why not?' agreed Thorgen. 'Plenty of travel, wassailing, looting and so on. Pity the training's a pain in the arse, eh?'

Athølred winced and nodded. 'I'm looking forward to knots.'

'Yeah, although I have to say I am dreading tomorrow's session on exchange rates. I was never any good with money. Still, two weeks time we'll be sailing.'

'I've never been to sea,' confessed Athølred.

'Me neither. I've been on a river, can't expect it'll be much worse than that. I mean, water's water, isn't it?'

'Any idea where we'll be going?'

'I've heard that Greenland's out.'

'Greenland?' Athølred sounded the unfamiliar word.

'Eric the Red discovered it a few years ago but it's miles away and not quite as green as he first thought. Now they're focusing on shorter trips, going for the higher turnover of sackable material. So it's got to be Normandy or Angleland. Can't stand the French, myself, bloody arrogant bastards—I'm hoping we're after the Saxons.'

And Thorgen proved to be right—two weeks later when the longboat pulled away from the wharf and let the tide ease her towards the estuary, the sail was hauled aloft and course set to the west. Bjorn moved through the boat collecting breakfast orders, although food was furthest from the recruits' minds as the ship yawed in the swell.

He laughed. 'You'll soon get used to it and believe me, no-one wants dead calm. Then you have to row and let me tell you, it's murder on your lower back.'

For sixteen days and nights they battled the driving winds of the Norse Sea, inching their way towards the coast of Anglia. Benny organised shipboard games and got a chess circle going but their spirits sank as the cold settled into their bones, despite much bloodcurdling yelling and manly slapping. It was with great relief one steely dawn that they welcomed the sight of the damp, flat and misty coast.

'What a dump!' said Thorgen, his arms resting on the oar as they stealthily made their way up a reed-lined tidal flat. 'It's nothing but a bloody bog!'

'Sshh!' hissed Bjorn. 'We don't want the Saxon curs to know we're here.'

'Hello?' murmured Thorgen to Athølred. 'A longboat filled with redheads and blondes that stand out like candles in a coal pit? Element of surprise, not!'

But nothing stirred in the marshes, the silence broken only by the splashing of oars as they dipped gently into the brine. The keel scrunched into the shingle and the longboat came to rest.

'Shoes off, everybody,' whispered Benny. 'Tie them round your neck and brace yourselves, the water's freezing.'

The raiding party, with daggers, swords and shields buckled to every limb, slid over the side and waded to shore. Patting their feet dry, they laced their sturdy boots and crept up the dune to survey the lie of the land. It was another dune, so they crept over that one, and the next, then the one after that before they had a change of plan and made their way along the nearby track that wound away from the sea. Smoke rose in the distance, so Bjorn hustled them into the low trees that crested a gentle rise. Hidden, they looked down on a Saxon settlement, its huts neatly arranged, livestock pens and tilled fields radiating from a central common.

'We'll eat well tonight, lads,' chuckled Bjorn. 'Now remember: this is your first trip, no silly buggers. We go in, we get out.'

'Anything we can sack?' asked Athølred, staring at the village hopefully.

'Can't say from this distance but I'd wager there's some fine manchester to be taken, maybe some pewter goblets, if you like that sort of thing. Personally I find them a bit too chunky for everyday use.'

'Bugger to keep clean as well,' said Benny. 'Right, let's light the flaming brands and get on with it. Who's got the tinderbox?'

The Vikings rummaged through their furs and checked their day-packs in vain.

'I think I might have left it on the boat,' said Thorgen apologetically.

'Brilliant!' muttered Bjorn. 'Next you'll be telling me you forgot the lunch boxes!'

Thorgen studied a nearby lichen intently.

'You did, didn't you? Well this is a good start! No, don't bother going back to the boat, we can do without the flaming brands but please, people, bear this in mind for next time: a raid looks much better with burning thatch, even in daylight. Alright, on the count of three, whoop.'

'Is that three and whoop or one, two and, whoop?' asked Englbert.

'Three and.'

'No worries. Three and.'

With beards streaming and flaxen hair tossing in the weak sunlight, the marauders broke from the cover of the copse and hurled themselves towards the village, waving their swords and whooping and yelling with a bloodcurdling ferocity. But the village remained silent. No Saxon heads emerged from doorways in alarm, no women and children ran screaming, no panicking old people conveniently fell over in the mud, and from their stalls the cows merely glanced at them, chewing their cud nonchalantly. Faced with such overwhelming indifference, the Viking charge petered out, their yells dying away to whispers that wouldn't curdle milk.

'Where's everybody gone?' asked Bjorn in confusion.

'It's only the animals left,' Athølred exclaimed, sheathing his sword.

'I am not raping goats again, I can tell you that for nothing,' said Benny flatly.

'No, no—the Saxons must be here somewhere,' said Bjorn, peering at the huts and outhouses. 'Unless it's market day and they're all at the shops—oh, that'd be right! The one day we turn up to pillage everyone's off snapping up the bargains!'

'Market day is Thursday,' came a stern voice behind them.

Bjorn turned to find a pike inches from his face, yielded by a tall yet stocky Saxon with hair as mousy as chaff. From every nook and cranny his countrymen emerged, spears and swords drawn, surrounding them with a ring of impenetrable steel. The raiders prudently dropped their weapons.

'Ah ... right,' said Bjorn, nervously forcing a smile. 'We'll come back—what was it, Thursday? Pick up a few things at the market then ...'

'Not so fast, stranger. Your face is unfamiliar. You're not from these parts, are you?'

'Er … no, we've travelled many miles across the …'

'Across the hills from the next county,' interrupted Benny, gesturing feverishly to the others to bite their tongues.

'That explains the regional accent,' conceded the Saxon, 'but your hair tells a different story.'

'We've been experimenting a lot with tones this season,' bluffed Benny. 'Mixing herbs for a longer-lasting shine, henna and woad, that sort of thing.'

From the beach, a boy came running. 'There's a boat ashore in the upper reaches of the estuary!' he yelled pedantically.

The villagers groaned. The Vikings exchanged nervous glances.

'Oh great!' said the tall Saxon. 'Just what we need: more bloody longboat people! This is the tenth this year. How many times do we have to tell you freeloaders? We will decide who comes to this country!'

'I've said it a hundred times, Beowulfin, we're just not sending out the right signals,' argued his offsider, a medium-height stocky man, his kempt hair the colour of chestnut with platinum highlights.

'I take your point, Athelguy, but deterrence takes time. One day these queue-jumpers will get the message: there are procedures to follow.'

'Excuse me, I'm sorry, ' interrupted Bjorn. 'You think we're refugees?'

'Of course—why else would you be here?'

'Oh, no, big mistake! We come from Trottingholm—do you know it? We're Vikings!'

'Vikings?' snorted Beowulfin. 'That's what they all say. Where are your flaming brands?'

'Er … they're back in the boat.'

'How convenient. And the pickled herrings?'

'Now I know this is going to sound lame and you wouldn't

credit it but they're back in the boat as well.'

'Silly me for asking. And what, the fishy stench, the filthy furs, the pillaging lust—that's all back in the boat as well?'

'Well, we like to floss, we try and keep the furs clean but if you want proof, we're happy to do the place over and rape your womenfolk.'

'Or you,' said Englbert eagerly. Athølred looked at him sideways.

'You can't fool me,' said Beowulfin. 'Your friend admitted your hairstyling secrets—you're no more Vikings than we are. Lock them up!'

Binding their hands behind their backs, the villagers poked and prodded the detainees along a rutted cart track until they arrived at an isolated stockade. They were bundled inside and given straw bedding and thin gruel, the doors locked firmly behind them.

'Well, this is good,' said Bjorn, sitting forlornly on his bed. 'Miles from nowhere, lousy food and the bastards think we're reffos!'

Benny, who had bagsed the top bunk, remained philosophical. 'Look on the bright side—they've got a pool.'

'Which means we're stuck in here till summer if we want to use it.'

'I think we should escape!' cried Athølred with a blood-curdling yell.

The others feebly echoed with a half-hearted roar. 'They've impounded our boat, impetuous youth,' said Bjorn in a slightly patronising tone. 'Even if we get through the bolted doors and past the armed guards, where would we go?'

'We could build another boat,' said Thorgen with sly cunning. 'I managed to slip something past our captors. I have … Lego!'

'How many blocks?' gasped Englbert.

'Six!'

'Fabulous. It might be just big enough to carry your pea-sized brain!' said Bjorn, clouting Thorgen over the head with a bolster. 'How can we prove to them that we're only here to set fire to a few houses, slip the odd maiden a firm one and then head off with the dinner service? It's not like we want to take out residency or get health benefits.'

'Could one of us get pregnant to appeal to their humanity?' asked Nils.

'We're all men. I'm no expert but I don't think that's how it works.'

Bjorn's musings were interrupted by the door creaking open. A thin Saxon, his hair the colour of hair, stood on the doorstep beside a guard.

'It's alright, Bardolph, I can take it from here,' he said and walked into the strongroom as the guard closed the door behind him. 'Well, you're in a fine pickle and no mistake. But fear not, help is at hand. My name's Erold, and I represent Concerned Saxons and Angles for Social Justice, or CAASFSJ as we like to call it to make things a bit easier. This is a contact visit, or a CV as we like to call it, and my role is to facilitate your appeal proceedings.'

'We just want to go home.'

'I understand you're feeling traumatised but I think there's a good chance we can get you a TRV, or Temporary Residence Visa, as we like to call it,' said Erold, momentarily confused.

'But we don't want to stay,' insisted Benny. 'We're a sea-faring band of Danish raiders, the idea is we land, get what we want and then leave.'

'You're not seeking asylum?' puzzled Erold, consulting his notes.

'Do you think anyone in their right mind would seek asylum here? Er …. no offence,' added Bjorn hastily.

'But can you prove you're from Danemark?'

'I have Lego,' offered Theogard.

'And we have flat-pack furniture in our boat—of course we're Nordic,' pleaded Benny.

'Well … I think we should at least have a case-officer run some background checks.'

'I tell you what. We'll pay a ransom!' said Bjorn with a sudden brainwave. 'We'll give you a Tor bookcase, a Knut storage system and a set of shelves called Loewbro, an incredibly flexible solution. I'll even throw in a set of allen keys. All you have to do is let us burn something—look, it can even be something you don't really need any more—then put a few platters in our sack and we'll be out of your hair on the next tide.'

Erold frowned. 'Hmm. I'll have to talk to Beowulfin. Meanwhile, avail yourselves of the facilities. We have a selection of magazines and there's a handball court out the back.'

Two days later, the raiders were taken back to the village. Beowulfin sat before the council of elders.

'We accept the terms of your ransom,' he said. 'But before you leave, you must assemble the shelving—the instructions are all but useless. Then you may burn Swithin's byre because he's building a new one and that will save him much effort, then take these unwanted wedding gifts of a fondue set and serving platter and leave our shores.'

'No how's your father?' asked Benny hopefully.

Beowulfin fixed him with a hard stare.

'Absolutely,' said Bjorn hastily. 'Thanks very much, can't say we've enjoyed it but if you're ever in Trottingholm, do drop in.'

And with that, the Vikings hurried back to their boat and with heaving oars slipped away into the Norse Sea. The Saxons watched them until the longboat dropped out of sight.

'There,' said Beowulfin with a smile of satisfaction, 'our borders stand protected. I told you, Athelguy, our policy is the right one. None shall cross this line we draw in the shingle.'

'Not even the Normans?'

'The Normans? Ha! I'd like to see them try!'

AD 1298

The merry green men of Sherwood

The dying sunlight dappled through the woodland trees as the anxious traveller hurried along the rutted cart track, eager for the safety of hearth and home. Years ago these woods had crept across vast swathes of the land, blanketing hill and dale, but centuries of felling had left little but pockets of the once mighty forests. Yeomen and peasants had cleared their small holdings, countless sturdy oaks had fallen before the axe to feed the hungry naval shipyards, and an export woodchippe industry had razed whatever was left of the thickets and groves where once sported the badger and lesser stoat.

Yet Sherwood Olde Growth Forest remained, a dark forbidding sentinel fighting a vain rearguard action against the relentless march of progress. Few men knew all its paths and valleys, nor the secrets held deep within the ash and alder copses. The traveller, weary after a sales conference in the local market town, now rued his decision to take a shortcut through the western fringe of the forest. He'd heard tales of bands of itinerants living deep within the shadowy woods, luring innocents who passed into their secret lairs, never to be seen again. An endangered splay-mouthed owlet suddenly swooped over his head and the traveller stumbled, wide-eyed with fear.

A man clad in green dropped from the lowest branch of a towering elm, then, springing to his feet with a deft, almost balletic plié, drew his bowstring taut and called, 'Halt! Stand and deliver!'

'Robert of Launceston!' cried the traveller in alarm.

'Aye, Robert Brown am I!'

'Fierce campaigner for social justice who has defied the laws of the land and donned the cloth of green!'

'Aye, the cloth of green.'

'And taken refuge with his fellow merry men in the last remnants of Sherwood Olde Growth forest,' stammered the traveller, his eyes fixed on the unwavering arrowhead, 'to fight against the evil King John!'

'You seem to know a lot about me,' said Robert, suddenly wary. 'And yet I know little of you. Your name, sir?'

'Bevan, my liege, a humble traveller in soft furnishings.'

'You're not a spy, are you, Bevan? If that's your real name…'

'"Tis the name my mother gave me, sir. No spy be I—I've just read about you in the papers, that's all,' muttered Bevan lamely.

'Mmm. Did you see the profile piece in *The Times*? I thought little of it, made me sound pompous. But at the end of the day, it's not about personalities—all of us in green fight for social equality.'

'To rob from the rich and give to the poor?'

'Well, yes', conceded the lanky outlaw. 'There has to be some sort of redistribution of wealth but I'm uncomfortable with those terms per se. This is not about us and them. This is about sustainability and frankly, King John can't see the bigger picture. Our fragile island cannot withstand the abuse we inflict upon her. We have to think beyond Nottingham, beyond these shores, link up with other eco-friendly outlaws and draft some sort of workable timeframe for a series of initial discussions …'

'Er … shouldn't you be tying my hands and leading me blindfolded to your secret hideout?' ventured Bevan.

'Ah, right. Yes. Good point. But 'tis only the draconian surveillance laws enacted by the evil sheriff that make me do it,' said Robert, binding his prisoner's arms with crocheted wraps and slipping an organic cotton mask over his eyes. 'And they have the gall to call this a democracy?'

'Actually, it's a one-party state ruled by a despot.'

'You said it, sister!' cried Robert, accidentally crushing an endangered Sherwood Bell-frog as he marched off through the undergrowth, dragging Bevan along behind him. 'And now we're the only legitimate opposition, the only political force that can make a difference, stop the rot and return control to the people. Well, not that they had control in the first place but for the sake of the argument, let's redefine our positions…'

Several sermons and a diatribe later, they reached their destination. From beneath his blindfold in the silence that fell when Robert stopped speaking, Bevan could hear the sounds of gentle industry; weaving, basket-making, the manufacture of amateurish and impractical ceramics. The scent of herbal tea and a more pungent aroma, as if of smouldering hay, drifted beneath his nostrils. Then with a wrench the blindfold was pulled free, and Bevan stood there blinking.

'Your camp!' he cried.

'Well, I prefer to call it a lifestyle choice but no, I've never made a secret of my sexuality,' said Robert, grabbing a hoe and quickly weeding the spinach bed in the large permaculture garden laid out to maximise sunlight.

'What about Maid Marian?' asked Bevan, running to keep up as Robert strode towards the rainwater tank to fill a rustic bucket and untangle a set of windchimes that dangled uselessly from a weathervane carved in the signs of the zodiac.

'She has issues,' conceded Robert. 'But Will Scarlett and I have made a commitment—that's why we'll fight to our last breath to change the draconian superannuation laws for same-sex partners.'

A slight figure clad in green with a cerise wrap emerged from the craft shelter and tugged at the rugged outlaw's sleeve.

'Robert,' he said gently, 'some of the lads want to fight for the rights of Wales.'

'End whaling, say I!' cried Robert.

'No, silly. Wales! Myth-wrapped land of leeks and eisteddfods.'

'Ah, right. Set up a steering committee, Will, and seek indigenous representation. We'll need someone to sign proceedings for the deaf and have ramps built for the mobility-challenged.'

'Meanst thou Steven the Legless?'

'He be the one. Contact the Conway Brothers and Margeret Roadknight and organise a benefit concert. Mysterious Wales is the land of massed voices—see if the Gay and Lesbian Choir of Bobbin Head are available. We can't pay anything but they'll feel better about themselves. And I want a Free Wales poster wrapped round every tree in the forest by sun-up. Recycled paper, of course.'

'And here's a sample pair of our new tights,' said Will, holding up shapeless leggings that looked like they'd been knitted with oars by blind sailors in the dark. 'They're made from hand-spun organic soya beans. One size doesn't fit all.'

'Soya beans?' asked Bevan with raised eyebrows.

'Little John kept smoking our hemp tights,' explained Robert. 'Painful when you're still wearing them. Ah, speak of the devil, here's Little John now.'

Bevan turned as the gentle giant emerged from the green-house. He'd been repotting some cuttings, a group bio-diversity project that had so far yielded some interesting varieties of lentils, onions and lima beans, the outlaws' staple diet. Eventually the greenhouse gases had proved overwhelming so Little John had sought fresh air.

'What-ho, Robert. I have news of the folk festival. King John has banned mead within the enclosure.'

'Sod that for a game of soldiers! We'll feast heartily on the special mushrooms before we go—what be the point of folk music without an altered mental state?' Robert turned his attention back to the tights. 'Yes, these will do nicely, provided the rain holds off. Will, tell Friar Tuck to order two dozen in Tuscan olive.'

'You have a priest?' gasped Bevan.

'Ex-Christian Brother—but we ask no awkward questions in the fellowship of the green. We just keep him well away from the creche.'

'You have a creche?'

'Absolutely! Every child-bearing woman has the right to a full-time career as an outlaw. The future of open social revolution can only be assured by getting the balance right between childcare and rebellion-related work commitments.'

Suddenly the clearing was filled with an acrid smell which seemed to emanate from a brown-clad, tonsured figure waddling into view. 'Robert,' puffed the noisome Friar as he drew near.'News of the compost! The worms have turned and the whole thing's a heap of shit!'

'Excellent! A job well done. Friable organic material is the gold all men should seek, not the tawdry gewgaws of the marketplace!'

As the Friar beamed and merry men jostled around him in manly congratulation (perhaps a little too manly at times), Bevan turned to Robert with eyes shining brightly. 'Robert— let me join you!'

'Well, normally we require two nominees and a cooling-off period—it might not work for us, it might not work for you and basically we've all got to feel comfortable. But I like your style and you've already got your own tights which is a bonus. Alright. Twenty shillings buys you membership and non-executive voting rights but you must do at least two working bees a year. Come, pull up a log! Little John, bring forth the tofu I-can't-believe-it's-not-beef and let us wassail!'

And so they sang, long into the night, dreaming of a better world as the campfire gently pumped 46.2 kilograms of carbon dioxide into the cold, starlit sky.

AD 1305

The Dark Ages

Flurries of snow, whipped by a cruel wind off the North Sea, skittered across the stonecutting yard as the master builder strode down the clinker path, his clerk tottering in his wake. He stopped before a man squatting on the ground, chipping away at a block. 'You, mason!' he barked. 'What are you doing?'

'I'm cutting a keystone for the crypt vaulting, my liege.'

'And what about you?' the master asked of another fellow.

'I'm carving a gargoyle's wing, sir.'

'And you?' he enquired of a third.

'Me, sir? I'm building a cathedral!'

The master builder turned to his clerk. 'You see? That's the kind of attitude we need!' he cried, giving the proud mason a turnip. His clerk sighed inwardly. No doubt the crawling toady had been to a seminar where mountebanks filled his head with motivational nonsense about releasing the power within. Probably couldn't build a cupboard, let alone a cathedral.

The clerk followed the master builder into the site hovel, a miserable lean-to that doubled as the works office and cesspit.

Warming his hands over a lump of smouldering peat, he braced himself for the morning debriefing. They'd been building this cathedral for over a hundred years—well, not they exactly, five generations of the clerk's forebears had toiled on the site; two had been crushed by falling masonry, one died of fresco poisoning while another had seen St Sebastian in a vision and become a nun. No mean feat, seeing he was six feet tall and a carter all his life. Even so, all that had been built to date were three walls and a cloister, and that was still missing the windows and latrine fittings. What was so difficult about a dozen handles and two rush lamps? The hardware industry had gone to the dogs.

'So, what news of today?' asked the master.

'We've had to stop work on the north apse. The flagstone layers' guild has called a wildcat strike and we can't get a slot in arbitration until next autumn.'

'Bloody guilds—they're ruining this country! What's the problem now?'

'It's an occupational health and safety issue. Apparently the magic tubers you gave them to ward off the plague didn't work.'

'Did they soak them in elderberry juice? That's the important bit.'

'I think they soaked themselves. Anyway, the ones that can still talk say the marble we got last month was just granite with swirls painted on it.'

'Bloody Italians—I knew we couldn't trust 'em! Saving all the best stuff for St Peter's and sending us the crap. Sooner we have a reformation the better. Anything else?'

'Well,' said the clerk slowly, 'we've had an injunction from the council. They've had an objection lodged against the belltower. It's going to compromise solar access for the residents in Butcher's Row.'

The master builder went off like a top. 'What? It's the bloody climate of this two-bit island that compromises solar access! If they want sunshine let 'em move to Byzantium! We are trying to build a cathedral, for God's sake!'

'Er ... indeed. But you know how these things work—once one person puts a thumbprint on an objection form, the council's got to act. And now they've got the National Trust involved. Seems that the church we knocked down to lay the foundations for the sacristy had significant Saxon filigree work on the door jambs.'

'We didn't knock it down, it fell down. It was made out of reeds held together with manure when Adam was a boy! Tell 'em we'll put up a plaque.'

'And we still haven't resolved the easement issue with the farmers beside the southern transept. They say we're restricting vehicular right-of-way to their meadows.'

'Meadows? It's a bloody bog! The only thing they can grow there is mould. Stupid peasants!'

'Oh, and they also object to you calling them peasants all the time. They'd like to be known as Indentured Vassals. It's a respect thing. Moving on,' said the clerk quickly, 'I think we've found the money to build the Chapel of the Blessed Virgin behind the high altar.'

The master looked up with something vaguely resembling a smile on his face. 'Good news at last,' he said.

'Ah ... yes and no. Squire Lance de Boyle is willing to contribute if we dedicate the chapel to his lady wife.'

'Have you lost your senses? She's had six children, eighteen if you count the ones that died—and you want her name on the wall of a chapel for the Virgin?'

'There's a bit more to it than that. We'd have to call the whole thing the Chapel of the Blessed Enid,' spluttered the clerk, ducking neatly to avoid a hassock being thrown in his direction.

'Forget it! Don't they realise what we're doing here? We are raising a house of worship to the Supreme Being, a glorious edifice filled with light and devotion thrusting heavenward, held aloft by soaring pinnacles of stone touched by the very hand of God himself!'

'Yes, but it's just that the hand of God has been a bit tardy with the building financing payments,' quipped the clerk lamely.

'Then why don't we put in a few apartments and retail space?' scoffed his boss.

'Well, it worked for the Vatican.'

The master grunted. 'Alright,' he sighed in resignation. 'I'll go to the Abbey and see if Father Back can convince Father Off to sell a few reliquaries. And I know he's got a few dozen pieces of the True Cross, they might raise enough gold for the rafters. And maybe—just maybe—we can think about a Choir Stall of the Blessed Enid.'

Meanwhile, twenty miles away across the fens in the market town of Cambridge, the Dean of the university stuck his head out of the sedan chair to find out what the hold-up was. It was ridiculous; 1305 and the traffic still moved at a snail's pace. Ahead he could see an oxcart, which had come to a complete standstill as the dozy ruminant strained with the effort of having two stomachs. The driver sat there straining with the effort of having one.

'Stupid oaf,' fumed the Dean. 'Doesn't he know this is a transit lane between Matins and Lauds? Two pigs and a duck do not constitute a passenger. Typical—you can never find a beadle when you need one!' He shouted to one of the dullards carrying his chair: 'Can't you go any faster?'

'It's gridlock, guv'nor. The town crier didn't mention any of this in the traffic round-up. We'd be quicker walking.'

'You *are* walking, you idiot!'

'Oh. Well, that should save us a bit of time.'

The Dean pulled his head back in, muttering about the state of the education system. He was crotchety from lack of sleep, having endured his wife's midnight attack of St Vitus' Dance, her legs thrashing and arms flailing. Honestly, the wretched woman caught whatever was going. Dawn had brought no improvement; as he'd sat and waited for his break-fast, she'd been hit by the dropsy and collapsed in a heap, upsetting the gruel pot and all but extinguishing the peat fire. On top of all that, he had a pile of unmarked exam papers to get through and still hadn't found a tutor for first year Aramaic.

He buried himself in the folds of his tattered cloak, strain-ing to ignore the odour that drifted up from the collar, an unsavoury reminder of the contents of his neighbour's cham-ber pot that had drenched him as he walked out his front door. Or strictly speaking what was left of his door, the deathwatch beetle having eaten most of it and the carpenter he'd arranged to replace it having died of something or other the day before he was due to begin. Honestly, it was nigh on impossible to secure a good tradesman; they always had some feeble excuse like premature death or being dragged off against their will to liberate Jerusalem.

'Would you like me to try my short cut, sir?' asked the chair handler, poking his louse-ridden head through the window.

'Does it involve going via London?' asked the Dean sarcastically.

'Ah—you know it then.'

'Take the next left turn.'

'And ... left would be on which side?'

'The side I am about to thrash,' snarled the Dean, taking out a crop and beating the fellow on the elbow. With a yelp, he picked up his end of the chair and turned left, coming to an abrupt halt behind a hardware wagon laden with cloister latrine handles and two rush lamps, its stationary wheels festooned with cobwebs and parking violation vellums.

The Dean groaned. Now he'd be even later for his lunch with the Alms Controller. Jesu, how he loathed this annual cap-in-hand grovelling for money. How could anyone be expected to run a beacon of educational enlightenment in this dark and ignorant age without assured adequate funding? Instead of teaching—or *scholastica interfacum* as the department insisted on calling it these days—he spent most of his time hunched over a parchment working on the budgets. The private money all went on raising armies and elaborate jousting matches. The king's much-vaunted Hex Scheme had been a complete disaster; even the threat of being cursed by a coven of witches did little to make the students pay up. Most of them just buggered off to the Sorbonne to study the songs of Courtly Love, desperate to become troubadors because that's where the real money was—and the women. Some even threw their wimples at you on a good day.

Not that the Dean understood modern music, all this two-note polyphony rubbish, banging their tabors so you could hardly hear yourself speak over the racket. Hildegard of Bingen; now that was music, all melody and no beat.

Many hourglasses later the chair pulled up outside The Rutting Stag, one of a chain of cheap taverns that specialised in merchants' lunches. Predictable choice of a petty bureaucrat, thought the Dean, his mood blackening as he passed through a venerable bead curtain into the dingy chamber. What's the bet he's ordered us the quarter-haunch of venison and a basket of fried beets?

The Alms Controller rose to greet him. 'I've ordered us the Quarter 'n' McMangels.'

'Marvellous,' toadied the Dean.

'Lucky I'm here, actually. Thought I was coming down with a touch of plague this morning but it seems to have cleared up.'

'Ah. I might just sit on the other side of the table, if that's alright.'

'Absolutely, Dean. Now, straight down to business. You know as well as I do that the king is dedicated to quality higher education but frankly, we're a little sceptical about the university's ability to deliver the performance outcomes that industry is looking for.'

'What industry? We're a feudal agrarian society working a three-field system because that's as high as your average peasant can count without haemorrhaging. It takes us two hundred years to build a church—you can hardly call that industrious.'

'Still,' said the Alms Controller, stopping himself from ogling the cross-eyed wench who brought their food to the table. Buboes aside, she was a bit of a looker. 'We believe that to get the most out of our educational florin we need to refocus on vocational training.'

'I don't think the university can offer degrees in how to gut pigs or pick chestnuts,' snorted the Dean.

'But are your students jobbes-ready?'

'A university isn't about jobbe training, we explore the intellect and push the boundaries of human understanding.'

'Well I'm afraid that's not what business wants.'

'Business? What the hell is business?'

'It's a new term,' enthused the Controller. 'Covers all those in commerce and great enterprise, it's the very ... er ... water-wheel of the nation's economy.'

'You want me to run a higher institute of learning catering to the whims of ... shopkeepers?' said the Dean, aghast.

'Frankly, yes. A range of careers has opened up with the introduction of the abacus and I know the Franciscans are on the lookout for high-end illuminators. Marco Polo's returned from the Orient—you could try for some foreign students from there.'

'They're hardly likely to know Latin or Ancient Greek.'

'Oh, I'm afraid all that humanities nonsense will have to go. Concentrate on physic, mathematica, that sort of thing. The first institute to map out the humours of the human body will be worth a packet, I can tell you. Might be a library named in the Dean's honour …'

The Dean's ears pricked up. 'Well, I suppose we could—I'll have to run it by the board, of course—but we could, perhaps, offer scholarships for … sporte.'

'Excellent start! Now, I'd offer you coffee but it hasn't been discovered. However, they do offer a very nice hot mud here. Tempted?'

AD 1491

Christopher Columbus
and the
new world order

In the year 1491 and a bit, the carrack *Santa Maria* rolled uneasily at anchor off the coast of Genoa. A blunt and stubby craft with an aft lateen rig, twin masts and another sail thing at the pointy end, she looked even less seaworthy than the leaking tender carrying Signor Umberto Quantacosta, accountant to Christopher Columbus, towards her. Umberto was no sailor but even he was beginning to doubt the wisdom of his master's grand scheme to discover a new world on the other side of the ocean.

He was hauled aboard and, picking over idle tars bored with endless days hove to, made his way to the stuffy aft cabin for the monthly project conference. Though not a tall man, he banged his head on the doorframe and inadvertently stepped into a cess bucket before finally reaching the comparative safety of an upturned barrel, the chairs having been sold off to pay the providores. Nodding to the others assembled around the table, he uneasily delivered his report and watched as Columbus stalked about like a caged tiger, hurling oaths from a vast glossary of obscenities accrued over a lifetime at sea.

'*Ay Caramba!* So what you're saying is, the trip's off?'

'Delayed, Christopher, that is all,' stammered Umberto.

'Delayed? Again? At this rate the English will discover the Americas before we do. What am I saying—the bloody Swiss'll be there first and they don't even have boats!'

Columbus kicked open a window and threw the ship's cat overboard for the fourth time that day. It swam back to the gunwale with a look that would curdle milk—if the expedition had had any milk; Columbus had thrown the ship's cow overboard three days before and it was last seen floating upside down towards Africa. 'We can't find anyone to back this enterprise, is that what you're saying?' he continued.

'The Portuguese are nervous,' said Umberto, 'there's just not the venture capital around anymore, especially after the collapse of juan.tell.'

'*Sacré bleu*!' snorted Columbus. 'Juan tell! Blind Fredrico could've told 'em that wasn't gonna work! How can anyone promise a Papal Emissary who can travel from Lisbon to Rome, get the edict from the Vatican, be back in under four months *and* throw in the scribe to illuminate your scroll for nothing? And they think we're crazy?!'

'They were going for the youth market.'

'You call that innovation? There ain't no other market, everyone's dead by 34—it's not like anyone's gonna make money selling pension plans!'

'Er, maybe we could get the meeting back on track,' said Stuarto Piccolomore, notary to the fiery Genoese sailor. He was a thin, acerbic man whose forebears had made a fortune bankrolling the tower in Pisa, although things got a little hot when they employed a wall-eyed surveyor because he was cheap. Luckily for the Piccolomore family, the tower contract included a non-perpendicularity escape clause and they avoided prosecution. Stuarto had kept alive the family tradition of innovative speculation by becoming a fellow promoter of Columbus's Viva Ameriga exploration and tax minimisation scheme.

'There are other fundraising avenues available to us,' he said. 'We could always approach the Ministry of Trade again.'

'*Bjåæøq!*' spat Columbus, which was a new one to all of them. 'That bunch of morons couldn't trade insults. And don't get me started with the forms they expect you to fill in—I don't even know my mother's maiden name so why the hell should they? D'you know the first thing they said to me? "We'll need a contact address for you in the New World." Hello? They don't have no addresses, the place is new—that's why they call it the New World, for Christ's sake! And these are the people we've got runnin' the country—half of them still think the world is flat!'

'Maybe we could get money out of the Vatican,' suggested Piccolomore.

'Doubtful,' said Umberto. 'They don't think the world is flat; they know it is. Plus they'd want a fifty-thousand pagan conversion guarantee up front.'

'And even though it was two centuries ago they still haven't made up the bundle they blew on the Crusades,' chipped in Don Corleone, a squat, shifty-eyed prelate from Sicily looking to expand his parish church's gaming interests into the new territories. Umberto didn't entirely trust him; since when did diocesan officials wear two-tone shoes and carry viola da gamba cases?

Rodrigo, head of corporate development, cleared his throat. 'There is some good news on the sponsorship front. Now I've always said investors like a high-profile operation and a fleet of ships is a lot more sexy than a single vessel, plus there's the feel-good factor, a much better chance that at least one of them can make it back …'

'You saying I'm goin' to sink my ship?' hissed Columbus ominously. In fact, far more ominously then he realised at the time.

'Er, no, not at all. But I think we now have two other ships lined up, the *Nina* and *Frederick* …'

'Frederick? *Cowabunga!* What kinda dumb-ass name is that for a ship?' barked Columbus, stabbing impatiently at the desktop with the sharp point of his dividers. Umberto winced; it was his desk—well, strictly speaking he'd leased it to the project from his personal super fund but he could see the resale value plummeting with every jab.

'Well, of course the name can be changed.'

'Too darn right it can. Anyone got any ideas?'

There was a thoughtful pause. The recently returned ship's cat sneezed. 'Well, we could continue the theme,' said Umberto tentatively. 'Call it the *Santa Barbara* …'

Columbus shrieked with laughter. 'Barbara? Sure—and why don't we call the other one Claus while we're at it?'

Umberto blushed. 'Barbara is my mother's name,' he said with wounded dignity.

'And a very nice name it is too, Umberto,' said Columbus, breaking the embarassed silence. 'But while you might have been grateful to spend nine months inside someone called Barbara, I can't see a hundred sailors being quite so keen.'

'Well, as a matter of fact,' said Rodrigo brightly, as always blind to a socially awkward moment, 'we've also secured naming rights for the *Santa Maria*—it's a minor alteration, just a letter here and there, but it could land us a major sponsor.'

'What've I got to change it to?'

'Er …. now try to think of this in gold paint with a nice font. It's, um, *Alfredo's House of Pizza.*'

'*Gott in Himmel!* Are you nuts? You want me to discover the New World in a boat called *Alfredo's House of Pizza?*' thundered

Columbus, now savagely gouging a two-foot scratch in the desktop with his sextant.

'But we get unlimited family-sized Supremes with optional anchovies—this could provision the entire expedition …'

'The pepperoni's gonna be growing secondary mould before we hit Gibraltar! What is it with you guys? You're my people; you're supposed to talk to *their* people and get this stuff sorted out. I'm gonna be busting a gut just steering the ship into the complete unknown—I mean, what is the point of having people if I gotta do everything myself?'

There was another uneasy silence. Columbus' personal assistant popped his head round the door. 'Just a reminder about your 12.30 to discuss artwork for the ship's log; the Lombards at 3.00 to go through your loan refinancing and your wife sent a message.' He consulted his slate. 'Pick up a butt of mead on your way home because the … I think it's the Castellis … are coming over and they might be good for a few thou. Does that make sense?'

Columbus nodded wearily and gazed out the porthole. 'You know, ever since I was a kid, I've been dreaming of the Indies. Marco Polo—he was an Italian, d'you know that? A Venetian boy, canal bandit. And I was always thinking, there's gotta be a way you can get to China like he did without having to ride a goddamn camel. Give me a caravelle and a star to steer us home … I could give you the world. But what have I got? An accountant who can prove nothing is possible, a lawyer who'd defend the Devil and sue God for the costs, and a fundraising team who couldn't raise their blood pressure at an all-nude revue. Get outta here, you make me sick.'

The project group rose to their feet, shamefaced. The ship's cat sneezed again.

'And for St Sebastien's sake, someone get the cat a god-damned handkerchief!'

There was the noise of a small boat heaving alongside then a messenger burst through the door. 'My liege, great news from Spain! An intermediary to Queen Isabella, Don Christolfo del Skasa, has brokered a deal with the royal court—the expedition is assured!'

The cabin burst into riotous cheering. Columbus was a man transformed. '*You bloody ripper!*' he swore. 'Spain! Now there's a country knows how to treat an entrepeneur!'

A short history
of sport

Netball is the oldest recorded sporting activity, a ball and a box-pleated tunic being found next to a plate of pikelets in a paleolithic grave site in Andalusia. Similar finds in northern Africa point to some sort of international competition table being in place by the first Ice Age, sports-archaeologists believing some of the larger caves in what is now Morocco could have been used as indoor venues when freezing temperatures made conditions outside uncomfortable. Indeed, there is emerging evidence to suggest that much of the 'secret women's business' of the indigenous populations of Gondwana 30 000 years ago was in fact a five-a-side netball tournament played between nomadic tribal groups during the dry seasons.

Why women first took to sport is anyone's guess, although theorists believe that having swept the caves, suckled the young and groomed the lice out of each other's facial hair, primitive women had time on their hands while the menfolk were away hunting large animals and bonding. Book-groups proved brief and unsatisfactory affairs, there being no books as such to discuss, so a game involving the throwing of a ripe melon from one to the other before slamming it through a hoop of woven willow fronds evolved. The game proved wasteful to the melon supply, a fresh melon being required after every slamming action, so the resourceful Neanderthals created a ball by filling a boar's bladder and covering it in stitched mammoth hide. Sadly, the small-brained primitives filled the bladder with boar's urine, from where we get the modern term to 'dribble' the ball, but nonetheless the game grew in popularity among the womenfolk until it was almost impossible to get a court on Saturdays unless you'd booked well in advance.

Halfway through the Meleotheolithic era, men discovered what the women were up to. They immediately accused the sport of lacking spectators, which was in a sense true—all the women played and the men were away running about the forest naked. Women were now marginalised as men seized control of the game, adding the use of feet, heads and full body contact in the manner that those challenged by their nascent sexuality seem to enjoy. Hunting was abandoned altogether until the men realised their tunics were practically falling off them, and it wasn't until the end of the second Really Cold Age that a sensible balance between hunter-gathering and sport was reached: one day hunting, six days sport.

By the third Precambrian Copper Age, interest in netball had dwindled. Lacking the frontal lobe development needed to make the imaginative leap to other forms of organised games, prehistoric man pursued more passive leisure activities like dried flower arrangements and snooker. It wasn't until 4000 BC that the Chinese discovered gymnastics, a series of delineated movements that displayed suppleness, agility and grace. It was a sport that suited the truncated lifespan of the time; a gymnast could retire at sixteen and die of old age three years later with the bulk of their career earnings still intact. In Egypt and Persia the sports of javelin, jousting and high-jump became popular, growing as they did out of martial activity, the javelin being obviously akin to spear-throwing and jousting to equestrian combat. What is less well known is that the high-jump reflects the Egyptian tradition of surrounding their battlefields with bars set at variable heights, over which the warriors leaped to prove their worth before joining the melee. If casualties were high, shorter, less-athletic warriors were permitted to limbo into battle to make up the numbers.

The Greeks really put sport on the map when Jonos Antonisis Samaranx declared, 'And the winner is: Olympia!' thus beginning a long and noble tradition of corruption, drug abuse and financial loss. The Games of the Olympiad were a chance for Athenian men to rediscover their love of public nudity, oil up and wrestle as the gods intended before a crowd of similarly interested men. They could hurl the discus, toss the javelin, run around in a circle or leap over things. Like Persia, Greek sport grew out of the military skills a soldier required and an ancient Olympian would scarcely recognise the Games today, little knowing the contemporary strategic importance of synchronised swimming or beach volleyball. But they would certainly identify with the hero status bestowed upon the competitors—well, at least the ones who win.

Across the seas in the Americas, the Mayan and Aztec peoples were ball-sports mad. Some of the stone playing courts they built for their hybrid form of handball are still in use today. To the north, the native American Indians were playing an early type of lacrosse, a game popular these days in English public girls schools like Mallory Towers and St Trinian's, while further north in the Arctic Circle, the Inuit whiled away the long winter nights playing darts and indoor carpet bowls.

With the collapse of the Roman Empire and the subsequent dampening effect on spectator ticket sales, the harshness of life in the Dark Ages that followed meant little recreational leisure time was available. Exhausted by long, backbreaking work in the fields, it was all most people could do to spend a few minutes in the evenings sorting out their stamp albums. Sport began to divide along class lines. If you were wealthy, you could afford to joust or shoot arrows at targets; if you were poor, well, you just had to be the targets. Fairs and feast days proved exceptions and on these social celebrations there's evidence of organised games: catching the greased pig, catching the greased wench, tossing the greased dwarf and so on. Footraces and tests of strength were popular, while boxing matches were organised by furtive men in fedoras behind the sheds handing out betting slips.

In the Tudor and Hanoverian periods, sports developed as an extension of the survival skills of the ordinary people. Fishing, long regarded as a tedious but necessary form of food gathering, was revolutionised by the introduction of the concept of 'throwing it back' and large numbers of men who'd do anything to get away from the kids formed angling societies, spending fruitless hours on damp riverbanks dangling poles over the water. The sport took another leap forward when fishing line was added to the poles and later additions of hooks and bait ensured its growing popularity to the point of unsustainability. Likewise hunting, once the domain of the rich and powerful, remained just that and inbred cretins armed to the teeth continued to blast the life out of small defenceless birds for no apparent reason. Royal tennis (so called because it was played by royals as opposed to lawn tennis which is played by lawns) stayed firmly within the realm of the English court, although squash was played in the Vatican and a crude form of badminton was enjoyed by the Swedes.

But it was the Industrial Revolution that changed the face of sport forever by allowing the emergent working class to join in. Team sports were largely a product of the industrialised West because the Lancashire mill owners quickly realised the sales potential in guernseys—a soccer team had eleven players, rugby fielded fifteen and in the colony of Victoria, eighteen got a run on the paddock in an AFL side. Sogby, a team game popular in the Bradfield area in the 1850s, had teams of fourty-eight a side who all had to change into fresh guernseys every fifteen minutes but the expense proved prohibitive to amateur clubs. Rugby league, the workingmen's breakaway code, clawed back the guernsey expenditure to thirteen and substitutes were permitted to share kit.

Cricket remained the dominant game of the middle and upper classes, only the well educated being able to make any sense of the stats. Test cricket became the only game in the world that could be played for five days without a definitive result. Protracted drawn matches soon eclipsed lesser-known spectator sports such as paint-drying watching and grass-growing observation. Golf, devised on the wind-blasted sand dunes of Scotland, quickly became an international sensation played largely by dull men with no dress sense. Deceptively simple, the sport requires a player to hit a small ball with a stick into a small hole some distance away. This is performed eighteen times before the players retire to a small building to drink and exchange business cards. Once a week, ladies are permitted to have the run of the course; at all other times, they are tolerated but not encouraged, the early netball wounds still running deep in the gender divide.

Of course, the mass popularisation of sport simply reflected the inner competetive nature of man but gradually this need to compete extended beyond the physical limitations of the human form. Soon any animal that could be raced found itself in a starting gate with a mildly deranged human strapped to its back. Horses, camels, donkeys, aardvarks—anything that had a half-decent chance of reaching the finish line without expiring was pressed into service. Bicycles, skates, sailing boats, canoes, planks of wood—Captain Cook observed indigenous Hawaiians surfing in the 1770s and discovered an extensive range of surfwear available in the shops when he landed on the islands. Mechanisation gave birth to motor racing and reckless daredevils would hurl around the track at up to fifteen miles an hour, stopping only for time in the pits, where highly trained crews could change the tyres and refuel the 'jalopies' in two hours.

Along with the growing emphasis on recreational sport there came a desire to simply sit back and watch other people making all the effort. Thus the professional sportsperson was born. The naturally gifted could command a high price for their services but sports organisers soon realised that a tournament played only by those who had a realistic chance of winning would be very short indeed. So to maximise ticket sales, they opened the competition to players who could only emerge as winners if everyone else fell over and broke something. Thus the professional also-ran was born.

On the back of this explosion of interest, many complementary industries sprang up. Umpires and referees needed to control the games were recruited from sado-masochistic societies, willing to dominate yet happy to be abused. The medical world learned to deal with the ubiquitous 'sports injury' and hundreds of physiotherapists who had studiously ignored men crippled in industrial accidents quickly set up shop to treat hamstrings and sprained ankles. Regulatory bodies attracted overweight, colourful identities with asthma to govern the codes and accept kickbacks from interested parties, while at the Olympic level, graft and corruption reached levels the Mob could only dream of. Agents and managers scrambled for their piece of the action—and why not? Suddenly any man who could kick a ball between two poles was being paid twenty times as much as the Nobel laureates who discovered DNA!

Sports journalism, which began as two lines of the Ascot results on the back page, relentlessly expanded at a rate that will soon see the back pages joining up with the front. Commentary teams were on air an hour after the first professional player retired. Initially, he simply talked to himself but soon other ex-pros joined him to rabbit on endlessly, as if in some way mysteriously qualified to pass judgement simply because they had played the game themselves. Like only Nazis could write the history of National Socialism! Cable and satellite TV meant that sport could be broadcast twenty-four hours a day on multiple channels; Methuselah could not live long enough to watch even the highlights packages.

Gymnasiums opened to get people fit for sports they would never play. Governments organised strategies to beat other governments in medal tallies and established anti-doping laboratories to catch athletes who were only trying to do what they were told to do: win. Spectators rediscovered sport's martial origins and began attacking each other, battle leaving the metaphorical playing field to be fought on the blood-stained terrace.

Sport became the opiate of the masses, a relentless addiction with more money pumped into its bottomless maw than the fight against global poverty, disease and famine. And why not? When was the last time you saw famine sink a forty-foot putt on a lightning green in a pressure play-off situation? I don't remember poverty seeing off the withering pace attack to post a solid yet graceful hundred by the tea interval. Disease has no chance of a breakaway run down the blindside, weaving majestically to put the pill right under the posts! And don't tell me a starving African kiddie doesn't dream of playing for his country, even if it is mostly for the oranges at half-time. Sport is the stuff of dreams, a metaphor for life! It's just a shame that most of our lives turn out to be a nil-all draw filled with unforced errors, played in the rain before a subdued handful of friends and relatives, an uninspiring tawdry affair that ends in relegation and a dud knee.

But hey, stuff it—pump up! Next time, we're gonna win, alright?

AD 1603

William Shakespeare applies for a grant

W illiam Shakespeare sat in a small anteroom in the Guildhall, anxiously awaiting his appearance before the board of Revels. The endless delays in his grant application gave him little chance of returning to his family in Stratford for the weekend. Quality time, his wife called it. Well, time it certainly was but the quality was debatable. He dashed off an apologetic note:

Twelve times the moon hath drifted on her path
Reminds me: 'tis high time I had a bath
I fear I'll not be home this Sabbath day
Foul deadline fast approacheth for my play
So could you pick sweet Hamnet up from school?
At eventide they free him as a rule
And from the cleaners, yea, collect my hose
Guess what? 'Tis said Marlowe was one of those!
All's well that ends Will (gets thou it?)

Secretly, he doubted that she would, and the iambic stress of the last line was a bit dubious but still, it would have to do—they can't all be gems, he thought. An attendant appeared and beckoned him into the adjoining chamber so with a sinking heart he rose to meet his fate.

'Ah! William Shakespeare—do come in,' said Sir Edmund, chair (relieving) of the Revels committee. 'You know everyone else, don't you?'

William entered the room and nervously cast an eye over the assembled artes personages. There were a few vaguely familiar faces but the only one he knew personally was Walter Grubbins, head of marketing and subscriptions at The Globe. At least Will could count on his support, although they had fallen out briefly when a party booking of fifty from Stratford had failed to show up for a matinee of *Henry IV*. Never again, Will had vowed at the time, will I attempt to organise a social function for any number greater than two.

'Now,' continued Sir Edmund, 'you're applying to the Revels committee for funding to underwrite a tour of ... er ... "Omelette"?'

' *Hamlet*, my lord, it's a play of mine.'

'And I see that this is the first time you have approached the nation's purse for moneys ... why so?'

'Well, my lord, I've never been pressed to before. I am but a man of the people and my pen writes to please the citizens at large. We rely heavily on the Office of the Boxe, and God be thanked that thus far the returns have been sufficient to our needs.'

There was a slow intake of breath from someone at the far end of the table and Will could just make out a muttered 'Too commercial, methinks!' He ignored the interjection.

'But this time,' he continued, glancing at his prepared notes, 'I was hoping we could set aloft our horizons and put together a package. You know the sort of thing; regional schools tour—maybe even Scotland if the cholera's not too bad— a couple of shows for the workers in tannery canteens, we can play the piece nigh anywhere. Maybe even a matinee for prisoners in the Tower …'

'Let's not lose our heads,' cautioned Sir Edmund.

'Ha! Nice one, your lordship! Tower—heads!'

His lordship stared blankly. Having only recently come from public works, he knew little of the world of showe business and was far happier with open latrines and earthen ramparts. His single experience of the stage had been performing the roles of Third Shepherd and half of the donkey in his grammar school's production of the Wakefield Mystery Play. Sir Edmund's wife, however, was a social climber and an amateur madrigalist, a minor talent that was thought sufficient by association to secure him the post at the Artes Counsel.

'My difficulty is, William, our complete shortage of money. This year alone we have to fund a Low Countries tour of Magna Carta: the Exhibition, take the king's singers to Wales *and* find the change to buy eight sackbutts for the royal horn section.'

'Hamlet was a big hit in London,' protested Will.

'So I'm told. I'm afraid I didn't see it, I rarely travel south of the river, but my real problem is this: we musn't be perceived as being London-centric. There are regional political sensitivities. Not that our artes funding is in any way political,' added Sir Edmund hastily. 'Strictly arm's length, of course, but the King needs to be reassured that the flow from the royal coffers is being, shall we say, channelled on a needs basis to clusters of artistic excellence.'

Being the greatest living playwright—certainly since Marlowe had been knifed in a tavern, or spirited away to Italy, depending on which out-of-work player you listened to— Shakespeare considered himself a cluster of artistic excellence but thought it prudent not to pursue the point.

'And we must satisfy ourselves that your play meets

the guidelines,' continued Sir Edmund.

'Guidelines?' asked Will suspiciously.

'There has been an internal departmental review and a framework of guidelines has been implemented. None of us want the artes to be seen as elitist.'

'Of course not, sir. Perish the thought that we strive simply for the elusiveness of excellence.'

'Indeed,' said Sir Edmund slowly. 'To wit, our asessment panel this morning have a few reservations about your play. Tony and Toni—perhaps we could start with you?'

Will's spirits sank. Now he recognised the pair with the close-cropped hair and enormous ruffs: Tony and Toni, chairpersons of the Southwarke Gaye and Lesbian Collective and two of the world's most humourless people. They'd noisily objected to the sexual stereotyping in *Coriolanus* and had organised a boycott of *Two Gentlemen of Verona* on the spurious grounds of misleading advertising.

'Personally, I'm insulted by the untimely death of Rosencrantz and Guildenstern. It sends a negative message about same-sex relationships to the community,' said Tony.

'Rosencrantz and Guildenstern are merely friends …'

'Hello? They go practically everywhere together and blow upon recorders! Just friends? Methinks not!'

'And I resent the cheap innuendo of Fortinbras,' chipped in Toni. 'Many women have fought in bras and you demean the vital contribution they make to the armed services.'

Shakespeare was taken aback and tried to lighten the situation with a quick jape. 'Yea marry, Tony,' he laughed. 'I bet you pack quite a big hose in that doublet, what?'

'Mr Shakespeare!' hissed Sir Edmund. 'You do your cause no good, sir, with intemperate sexual innuendo. Kindly remember this is a workplace!'

'Pardon, my lord,' murmured the Bard sheepishly.

'I represent the English Tourism Board,' said a man dressed in red, white and blue. 'And I'm outraged that the whole thing's set in Denmark! If you want taxpayers' money to support a local drama industry, then give us English stories, not this load of rubbish about miserable sods in Elsinore. While we're at it, what about *Twelfth Night*—why couldn't you set that on the Isle of Wight?'

'With all respect, sir, Illyria is an allegorical land. And one, perhaps, more exotic than the Isle of Wight. Mind you, were it set there, Orsino could always use this one: what's brown and steams out of Cowes backwards?'

'I know not, sir!'

'The Isle of Wight ferry!' said Will, the smile freezing on his lips as he looked at the stony faces confronting him. Even Walter Grubbins remained silent, although in his defence he had heard it before.

'A jape every bit as funny as the impenetrable tripe you put into the mouths of your buffoons and clowns, Mr Shakespeare,' said Sir Edmund acidly.

'That's satire, sir, it's not supposed to be funny,' protested Will lamely.

'Mission accomplished, I'd wager. Does anyone else wish to say something?'

'*Hamlet*'s very long,' came a quavering voice. 'Many of the senior citizens I represent have trouble getting back to their hovels in the dark, especially now they've cut out the subsidised carts for self-funded retirees.'

'And where's the mention of farmers?' said an odd-smelling man who sat slightly apart from the others. 'We pay tithes just like anybody else. All very well for you city types with your courtly ways—what, don't they have farms in Denmark? Even a couple of pigs on stage would be a start.'

'I think there's talk of an orchard in Act One,' stammered

the beleaguered playwright.

'Well it went straight over my head, sunshine. And I didn't think much of Ophelia either. Looked like a bloke.'

'Er … the actor was a bloke.'

'Typical!' muttered Toni darkly.

'Look,' said William with growing desperation. 'I can fix all this with a few simple re-writes. I'll rename the play "Hamlet: Prince of Bournemouth", we'll make his mother Gertrude a repressed lesbian …'

'Not much of a stretch with a name like that,' conceded the rural representative. Toni shot him a withering look.

'Er … Polonius has an interest in corn threshing, Horatio's on the pension and we lose Act Four …'

'That's all very well,' said Sir Edmund, 'but at the end of the day the play hardly does a lot for the image of kings, does it?'

Shakespeare looked confused. 'I'm sorry, my lord—the other changes I can live with, but I don't think the play will stand without Claudius as a murdering usurper to the throne.'

'Exactly. So I'm afraid that on behalf of our sovereign and benefactor, he who signs the cheques, I'll have to inform you the answer is no, Mr Shakespeare. Do I make myself clear?'

William sighed as the penny dropped. 'Yea, Minister. Crystal-like.'

AD 1666

The diary of Samuel Pepys

FEBRUARY 23RD

The wife hath given me another diary for my birthday; purchased from the newly opened gift shoppe next the Tower, so right glad am I she bought me not a novelty beefeater! She could not resist, said she, there being a sale on all marked goods, diaries and year planners being so marked with another 15 per cent off. Yet I confess to growing weary of diary-keeping and had it not been for mine resolution of New Year, I would gladly desist. What to write? Weather continues poor, did not do much today. Hied me to the shoppes at lunchtime for the plague sales. Word hath it that the epidemic is fading, thanks be to God, the fearful toll on local services can scarce be calculated—the library hath been closed for a month. Returned home then took me a nap, whence had I the strangest dream! I dreamt my wife had given me a dairy, the Samuel Pepys dairy, and upon each cow there rode a small man, no taller than a hand. I must refrain from cheese ere I slumber. Turned in early.

FEBRUARY 24TH

Jesu, another diary entry to write scarce four-and-twenty hours since the last! Today much the same as before, though enjoyed we an hour of sun in the forenoon. Despite the chillsome winds, Mrs Pepys took to the garden to be baked by its rays, an indelicate practice to mine eyes but she listened not to me, par for the course when all is said and done, sometimes methinks I might as well be not here at all. Hied me to the shoppes, the butcher declaring Choppe Tuesday, so bought me a pound of same. No news from the Admiralty, I can but hope they received my résumé. Lord Sandwich hath written an excellent reference and I hope his patronage will find me favour with the King, although in truth, my noble benefactor has been distracted by his new culinary creation, meats and/or vegetables of salad pressed between two slices of bread. He calls it the Lord. It catching on I cannot see; likewise the Earl of Chutney's condiment. Took me to my bed early but slumbered not, mine twitchy legs chasing phantom sleep away.

MAY 7TH

Finally found my diary again, cannot say I hath missed it, but now perhaps the wife's nagging will cease. Fatte chance. The new scullery maid Elizabeth came across it in the salon, though what she was doing in there with the gardener escapes me, the salon being the domestic zone of neither. Pleasures of the flesh perchance, though long hath I suspected the gardener playeth ball for the other team. And Elizabeth be nothing to look at, fine bosom notwithstanding. Yet who can say where Cupid's arrow will fall, 'tis all God's mystery and that be the truth.

But I hath news to report. The King hath appointed me Clerk of the Acts to the Navy Board! My excitement could scarce be contained. Mrs Pepys knew not what had hit her when I suggested an unscheduled matinee in celebration. It be my duty to find Acts for the end-of-year Naval Revue at Portsmouth. Talent runs deep in the naval pool and I hath in mind the quartet of lively tars who gave a burlesque during the royal visit to Harwich; fine-voiced and saucy, with a good line in visual comedy. Need I as well an ingenue, novelty act and an artes personage of standing within the community to perform the national anthem. Writers need we as well, perchance Wycherley or young Congreve will pen a sketch. Sent I a letter of thanks to Lord Sandwich for his continued support, although I hear he has travelled to France to advise the Comte de Baguette on the snack-line market.

In the evening I dined with Carrington and Spencer; thence to the playhouse to see *Cats*. Carrington has witnessed the piece twelve times yet never tires of it, infatuated as he be with Mrs Johnson, the actress who betakes the role of Grisabella. Yea, truly she has the one decent song in the showe, but I was left cold on the whole, there being a mighty draught under my seat. Slept well, yet could not rid my head of the Jellical theme— hath I not heard it someplace else before?

JUNE 12TH
Glorious sunshine smiled upon our departure for Spitend and all were merry in the coach. Lord Sandwich, the Burgher of Calais and the Master of the Rolls made for delightful picknic companions. Truth to tell, betook me too liberally of the porter and pickled onions and thus banished was I to sit aside the driver but nought could dampen my spirits. We lodged that night in the tavern and were bedevilled by rude and bumptious ruffians—twice had I to summon the night porter to quieten the riot, slept I not a jot.

JUNE 17TH
Arrived in Spithead, having made excellent time. Thence to a

naval inspection and when the physick declared our navels fit, hied we to the docks to review the fleet. What greater sight in Christendom than His Majesty's navy lying ten abreast at anchorage! Doth fair Albion send forth a more pressing signal to the world of her might and majesty? The *Redoubtable* was fresh back from France and to spite the King's impositions upon beer, ale and other divers liquors, got we duty-free cognac full up to the allowance and a carton of fagges. A bottle we took to the lodgings of Mrs Coleman, a handsome woman of mature years, and much merriment was had with she and several fine ladies of her acquaintance. I must confess to being sorely tempted to set aside my marriage vows but 'pon closer inspection, the pox scars did put me right off and I contented myself with a rubber of bridge instead.

JUNE 18TH

Auditions continue apace. Laughed heartily at Beaumont and Fletcher, juggling double act, who presented themselves before me at Sir W. Pen's residence. Not that I find ought amusing in the art of juggling itself, but I was mightily tickled—nay, all but nigh wet myself—by the antics of the troupe's dancing bear; confused and tormented, the animal took leave of its senses, completely forgot the choreography, and betook a large chunk out of Beaumont's leg. Only the poor man's dying screams alerted us to the fact that the business was not intended, yet, as the fellow was dragged away to bleed to death in the hall, we could not prevent a chuckle escaping again from our lips. Mercifully, Fletcher could see the funny side and the untimely demise of his lifelong friend was made a little the easier to bear. No punne intended.

Reminded was I of an outing to Tyburn to witness the brigand 'Pistols' McGuire be hanged, drawn and quartered. He seemed resigned to his fate, waving to his supporters, yet with

God as his judge, the hapless executioner became confused in his ministrations, reversing his procedure and the villain was hanged at the last in four pieces by the neck, one arm and each leg. Luckily, his widow saw the funny side and joined in much laughter from the good-natured Bank Holiday crowd.

JULY 2ND

It is with much alarm that I must feign report the secrecy of my diary has been breached! Saucy scullery maid Elizabeth be my prime suspect, she hath taken a set against me since the incident in the linen press. I fear Mrs P may be privy to what then happened in the privy! So I hath a devious code invented, to wit: A im now writing thas an i secret code. At as brallaint! Mrs P wall never twag! On the morrow, A wall pliy maghtaly wath i siucy biwd!

JULY 3RD

A hive moodafaed the coode slaghtly. Noo siucy biwds is yet.

JULY 4TH

A im hivang troouble reidang the coode. As the i a oor the a i? Stall noot oone siacy biwd woorth daddly squit his pissed my wiy!

JULY 8TH

To the devil with the code! For good news; Elizabeth has died of the plague. Downe side is that we hath breathed her noxious contagions. I shall retire to my bed and eat nought but garlic and rosemary.

AUGUST 2ND

Nigh on a month hath I spent abed, with nought to show for it but the invention of Greek cuisine. I must write to Lord

Sandwich and inform him of same, though I hear tell he has ventured to Italy, seeking il Conte de Panini to learn the mystic art of toasting.

AUGUST 21ST

Took I my niece and her friend to the Southwark Faire. Mrs P did insist I spend quality time with the offspring of her brother; ground I my teeth and bore it, veritably martyred like good St Sebastian, save the arrows and the death. As we ventured south of the river, the weather turned inclement—aye, verily, they should hold Southwark Faire to break a drought. Methought the faire unsuitable for lasses of such tender years yet my fears proved ungrounded; no sooner had they hit the mead tent than screeching fishwives became they, rousting as good as any bawd or pander this side of Lambeth. Amongst the players, jugglers and mountebanks, I kept my eye keen for talent for the naval revue, full intending to claim this outing 'gainst my tax. And saw I talent of another kind aplenty, af you know whit A mein! Lost I full three shillings to a card sharp hawking Hunt the Widow on a rickety table next the coconut shy and God strike me if 'twere not my niece in disguise! I thrashed her soundly, retrieved my moneys then sent her back to work, splitting the take fifty/fifty on pain of revealing all to her father. Repaired we then to the refreshment tent for a brace of partridge, three guinea fowl, a side of beef and nine quarts of ale, then a quick roger of the serving wench light-horse fashion about the enclosure. Quality time indeed!

AUGUST 22ND

Am penning this entry in the doghouse, Mrs P having read of my last entry, as it were. Mary, sister of the foul maid Elizabeth (deceased), visited this morrow on pretence of collecting her late sibling's holiday stipend and shewed mine wife the offending pages. Strumpet. I am running short of ink and wi

SEPTEMBER 22ND

Mrs P has at last released me from the kennel and given me a quill to record the dreadful news—a fire has burst forth from a bakery in Pudding Lane, completely ruining the wholemeal loaves, the cheese swirls and threatening the City of London itself! We hath hastily packed up valuables—The etchings! cries Mrs P—Save the family etchings! Methought this could be a good time to lose the diary altogether but no, her indoors hath carried it forth, safe from the flames. Hurried we to the river to view the conflagration from safety, joining our fellow citizens in a good-natured gathering by the water's edge, with much oohing and aahing as another steeple fell amidst a torrent of sparkes. No doubt Wren will be busy scheming, there will be many contracts for reconstruction with ample margins for inflated charges. One's man snake of misfortune is indeed another's ladder to success! Oh, me wish I had said that. One moment—me did!

SEPTEMBER 26TH

By the grace of God our lodgings hath escaped the flames that burned full three days and nights; we hath lugged our goods and chattels for nought. My back is all but spent. The city lies a smoking ruin around us but good news is, the plague has been consumed by the flames, likewise Mary. Goode result all round, say I.

NOVEMBER 15TH

The naval revue has not been the glitt'ring night all had hoped for—in truth: a disaster. I know not what went wrong. The house scarce filled the front stalls, there being a printing error on the handbills. Our burlesque quartet, mainstay of Act I, numbered but three, Seaman Staines having been press-ganged o'ernight to serve in the Indies, and as he was the only one who could truly sing and dance a merry jig, his comrades were found sadly lacking. Mrs Campbell imbibed mightily of the port ere she sang the anthem, though before God I must report that 'sang' be not the correct word. His Majesty recognised it not, nor anyone else and thusly none stood for the royal personage. Be I mortified! The comic proved an unwitty dullard and many of the audience returned not after interval. Yet Lord Sandwich did a brisk trade at supper with his newest line from Araby, the pita pocket.

DECEMBER 25TH

Yuletide brings no cheer; the weather bitter cold and the standard pair of socks mine only gift. Still no news from the Admiralty so I must face the worst: the naval revue will not be touring. In truth, no surprise. I still awake from my slumber bathed in a cold sweat as I vividly recall the finale and the sight of Mrs Campbell, *déshabillé*, bidding farewell to her supper into the orchestra pit. I fear not e'en the intervention of Sir W. Pen can protect my position—it be the labour exchange for I. Hey ho. Hied me to the shoppes but they were closed, being a public holiday. Turned in early.

JANUARY 18TH 1667

The cat has gone to meet its maker. Mrs Pepys much upset, far too distracted to bury the wretched thing, so 'twas Muggins breaking his back in an attempt to break the frosty ground which yielded not to the shovel. Gave up same as a lost cause and threw the deceased into the next-door neighbour's midden, hastily cobbling together a cross and a pile of fresh-raked soil to pass as his final resting place. Mrs P none the wiser and become quite affectionate in her sorrow, Tiddles all but forgotten in afternoon sport. A rare and pleasant day for Samuel Pepys, Esq.

FEBRUARY 23RD
The celebration of my birth swings round again and bugger me:
another diary!

AD 1865

What the Dickens!

On a warm day in June 1865, a curious figure made his way along the Gravesend road, muttering to himself as he scribbled long columns of figures on a piece of grubby paper, at the head of which the words 'The Deal' had been heavily underscored. What weighty enterprise of finance engaged this peculiar person remains a secret, for glancing up at an imposing edifice that had presented itself in the shape of Gad's Hill, the home of the nation's most succesful novelist, the man hastily pocketed his worksheet, straightened his topcoat and presented himself at the front door.

Minutes later, he was shown into the library by a disdainful butler; funny, he thought to himself, how disdain seems to go with the job description. He waited, with an almost gleeful enjoyment of the glacial increments of social distinction for the servant to withdraw and when the door had closed with the satisfying thunk afforded by a twelve-inch jamb, he turned to the master of the house.

'Mr Dickens? Mr Charles Dickens?' he said ingratiatingly. 'Allow me to introduce myself. Mr Warner, of Warner and

Warner (Bros), publishin' house in the City—your 'umble servant, sir.'

The great author took the offered visiting card and looked imperiously at the obsequious figure before him nervously fingering the greasy rim of a battered top hat. Returning to his chair behind the vast leather desk, he straightened a commemorative copy of *Great Expectations* then looked meaningfully out the window. 'Tell me, Mr Warner, what brings you to Gad's Hill?'

'Hindeed, sir, hindeed. The question on everyone's lips!' said Mr Warner with a knowing wink and a sly glance around the room.

'Then pray affix an answer to yours.'

Mr Warner bent double with a bronchial guffaw, feverishly shaking his head and slapping his thighs, raising small clouds of dust from his threadbare trousers, before collapsing into a small tub chair. 'Ah, the wit, Mr Dickens! The wit!'

Alarmed, Dickens leant surreptitiously towards the emergency bellpull beneath his desk, installed to alert the servants to dangerous interlopers after a nasty incident; a distraught reader who had burst in, objecting violently, and with much discombobulation, to the length—and grammatical convolution—of a particular sentence within the chapter relating the untimely and unfortunate death of the smaller Dombey.

Wiping his eyes, Mr Warner straightened up and spoke. 'Forgive me, sir, just one of my little turns. I shall be myself within the minute, although I 'azard a small sherry may well speed my recovery.' When it was obvious no sherry, small or otherwise, would be forthcoming, Mr Warner ploughed on. 'I ventured 'ere, sir, with a financial proposition.'

Dickens' hand froze. Nothing arrested his attention more dramatically than an offer of a pecuniary persuasion. His last reading tour of the Potteries had been a shade less than triumphant—'Same old, same old' to quote the *Manchester Guardian*, a remark that still rankled. Let them try and write 640 pages of social commentary, let alone read it out loud for three hours before a gaggle of semiliterate dinner service manufacturers! He'd already spent the latest advance-against-royalties from his publisher and the house needed a complete new set of antimacassars. Perhaps it would be prudent, he thought, to let Mr Warner have his say. At least he's not asking for autographs.

'But before I henlighten you, sir, p'raps you could do me the honour of signing this for my daughter,' said Mr Warner, shooting his sleeve cuff and presenting it to Dickens for his signature. 'She's a huge fan, especially of the shorter chapters of *The Pickwick Papers*. Laugh? I thought she'd had a seizure!'

'Indeed,' said Dickens dubiously, but reaching for his pen nonetheless. 'But your words of a proposition intrigue me, sir.'

'Well, as you may know, sir, we at the Brothers Warner are a quality publishing 'ouse specialising in your niche markets—saucy yet tasteful seaside postcards, romantic novellas and the like. 'Owever, we 'ave recently hexpanded into the magic lantern business …'

'Enlighten me, sir. The magic lantern?' asked Dickens, relenting and offering his guest a modest beverage.

'Thank you, sir, much obliged. 'Ave you not seen it? Ooh, it's magical! 'Ence the name. Fundamentally speakin', it's a mechanical happaratus whereby through a series of lenses and such, a powerful candle projects pictures onto a screen, artfully combined with words to fill in the gaps, while accompanied by the pianoforte. The result—an hentertainment hexperience like no other! In our pursuit of morally edifying and spiritually upliftin' stories, we are combing the back catalogues of literary giants, such as your good self, for, shall we say, material suitable for adaptation to the tiny screen.'

Dickens barked with laughter. 'Strange flattery indeed, sir, to suggest that my work can be reduced to shadowy images projected onto the wall of the local Corn Exchange before a crowd of gaping yokels.'

'Oh, henlarged, sir!' protested Mr Warner. 'Your work would be henlarged!—if that were possible,' he added quickly. 'A picture speaks a thousand words and I hadmit, we'd need a few 'undred pictures for *Martin Chuzzlewit*—but I assure you, the magic lantern is not just for your yokels of the gapin' variety. True, our demographics do favour persons of less fortunate breedin' but, why, just last week we had the Duchess of Barnstaple in the very front row! At least, I think it were 'er, 'ard to tell with the veil and ev'rythin', but sir! think of the hopportunities!'

Dickens pondered. 'Well, there may be some worth in bringing my searing indictment of the Chancery courts to a wider audience, and many of the poorer classes remain illiterate, despite my pleas for adequately funded education, even of the most rudimentary nature. Surely, in a society that dares call itself decent, it is nothing short of a scandal that so many of our children walk the streets in rags, scarce able to recognise a letter, let alone write one …'

'Er, yes,' said Mr Warner, pointedly examining his fob watch. 'But a word of advice—I'd leave the gritty realism to the colonies in New South Wales, sir. Their local magic lantern business can't get enough tales of the socially disenfranchised. Can't get enough of an haudience neither, by all accounts. Which is why, sir, I was thinkin' of something the whole family can enjoy.'

'It's never too soon to inculcate a child with a sense of social responsibility, Mr Warner.'

'Hindeed, sir. But p'rhaps the Sat'day matinee is neither the time nor the place, if you'll pardon my French.'

'Hmm. I wrote a moving tale of Little Nell and her destitute grandfather, once owner of a curiosity shop, but swindled by a malevolent dwarf ...'

'Ah? Appealin' across a wide age range, something for the antique lover and the vertically challenged ... sounds 'eartening,' nodded Mr Warner.

'Until Little Nell dies in a tragic scene that would melt the most adamantine heart.'

'I don't doubt it, sir, but it leaves precious little hopportunity for a sequel. Could the grandfather go to meet his eternal reward instead?'

'I fear it may lack the same emotional power,' said Dickens testily.

'I see your point. Old geezer shufflin' off this mortal coil, 'ardly surprisin' news, is it? Could she die but it were all a dream? P'rhaps not,' added Mr Warner hastily, seeing the nervous tic developing in Dickens' left eyelid. 'Do you 'ave anything with 'ealthier children? Cheeky Cockney sparrow with a smile as wide as London Bridge?'

'What about *Oliver Twist*? Orphan boy flees the workhouse but falls foul of a gang of pickpockets run by Fagin, a self-serving Jew ...'

Mr Warner almost choked on his madeira. 'Please, sir, an unsympathetic Semite spells nothing but trouble with the anti-discrimination board!' he spluttered. 'And it's box-office death in Bethnal Green. I lost my shirt with *The Merchant of Venice*. Could this Fagin be Irish? O'Fagin, p'rhaps?'

'Well, yes—he's as good as hanged, anyway.'

'Mmm, maybe not in the second draft if he tests well with the audiences. Any love interest? Steadfast friend, loved as a sister, until the truth of 'er beauty is revealed? Or a prostitute with a heart of gold?'

'Nancy. She's beaten to death by a brutish lover who finds himself shot down by an angry mob.'

'Sounds hilarious.'

'I don't do *funny*, Mr Warner! Humorous, yes, but if you want a song-and-dance japester, I suggest you try the music hall!'

'My apologies, sir, I meant no disrespect. But I'm told you 'ave a tale of two cities—forgive me, I've not read the volume myself, I 'ave no time for readin', run off my feet, I am! But pray, what two cities might they be?'

'Paris and London.'

'Ah. Don't suppose they could be Leeds and Bradford, by any chance? Considerable savings on location costs.'

'I don't see how that's possible, seeing that the book is about the French Revolution!'

'Have they not had a revolution then in Leeds or Bradford?'

'Not unless you consider the Industrial Revolution, and that would make little sense of the guillotine—if you'll pardon my French,' said Dickens with a sneer.

'Correct me, sir, but I take it the book also ends with a tragic death?'

'But of course.'

'Hmm. Somewhat of a recurrin' theme, isn't it? Still, p'rhaps it's all for the best—between us, workin' with the French can be a nightmare! All very harty!'

'Hearty?' asked Dickens, puzzled.

'No, harty. "Igh-falutin'." Well, Mr Dickens, I'll put my cards on the table. With all respect, what we're really after is a— how shall I put it—a publishing phenomenon. Something that lends itself to ancillary merchandising—David Copperfield cruet sets, a Miss 'Avisham line of bridal haccessories …'

'But they're from different books.'

'Well, sir, the magic lantern business is not hafraid of a little judicious cut-and-paste. If you could put your mind to a tale of triumph over adversity, preferably by the under-tens, with the odd hobgoblin and the sympathetic star-crossed lovers brought to joyful union by a wizard, we can have the attorney sign the paper before luncheon. Promisin', I assure you, a very generous return for your good self.'

Dickens considered for a moment. 'Very well. You shall have a manuscript within the month.'

'Oh, don't go to too much trouble—a two-page scenario and some character breakdowns will be more than sufficient, sir. We 'ave our own people to fill in the gaps. Well, a pleasure doin' business with you,' said Mr Warner, rising from his chair and shaking the dickens out of Dickens' hand. 'Good day to you.'

And with that he stumped out of the library. The butler showed him to the front door and as he stood on the step, all but ready to depart, Mr Warner turned with a look of enquiry upon his face.

'Now pray, my good man. I'm after a Mr George Eliot. Hany idea where he lives?'

Another time
nowhere in particular

A short history
of opera

The words 'history of opera' provoke three immediate
questions: what is history? What is opera? Will any of
this be in the exam?

In the words of Henry Ford, history is bunk, although by
logical extension, Henry's opinion is also bunk because he
himself is history. Opera (the plural of the latin *opus*, a work, as
in 'What a turgid piece of opus this proved to be', the *Age*) is a
dramatic work set to music performed by singers accompanied
by instruments. It may be interspersed with recitative or
dialogue but preferably not. And for those taking the History
of Opera exam, yes, you will be questioned on the following
dissertation but the rest of you can get on with quiet activities —
no scissors.

Let's start at the very beginning, a very good place to start.
Claudio Monteverdi (1567–1643) is widely regarded as the
father of opera, although he vigorously denied it in court until
the judge pointed out that no-one was pressing another
paternity suit or demanding maintenance payments. His
predecessors Peri and Caccini had written quasi-operas

dominated by unaccompanied recitative but they proved to be as dramatically interesting as a nine-year-old (1599–1608) singing the dictionary. Monteverdi, ever mindful of artistic developments around him, exploited many of the various musical forms available in Venice in the early seventeenth century and invested psychological depth in his characters to produce sung narrative dramas with a beginning, a middle and an end, although in performance the three did not necessarily occur on the same day.

L'Incoronazione di Poppea (1642), his last operatic composition, remains the one most often presented today. However, twelve operas he had written earlier in his career in Mantua were lost when the city was invaded by Austrians who obviously weren't as keen on opera then as they are now. Fragments of one of those missing, *Il matrimonio d'Alceste con Admeto*, have recently been rediscovered in a shed in Vienna and musicologists have pieced together the libretto written by Monteverdi's brother, Ira. It's hilarious, in as much as anything written in the seventeenth century is hilarious (think Shakespeare's clowns) and gives an account of a Mantuan wedding reception. In Act VII, there's a deliciously wicked aria sung by the padre that targets the Vatican's profligacy under Pope Urban VIII. The aria goes for almost half an hour and while one can sense a modern audience perhaps growing restless during the fifteenth verse about how much damask the Vatican bought in the financial year 1629–30, I'm sure to audiences of the day, the satire of *Il matrimonio* cut deeply.

Alessandro Scarlatti picked up the baton (as it were) and ran with it, composing 115 operas between 1679 and 1725, when his career was cut short by an assailant who'd frankly had a gutful of them. My personal favourite is No. 78 (he'd given up on titles by that point), a blunt attack on the Greater Naples Municipal Council and their appallingly slow clearance rates for DA applications. Obviously venting one of Scarlatti's personal grievances, the work failed to find an audience, except for the second Saturday matinee, when a party-booking of disgruntled council employees appreciated the references and asked permission to perform excerpts at their Christmas party. Scarlatti refused until they offered him a case of beer for his trouble. He remained unfazed by what was otherwise critical indifference to No. 78; by that time No. 79 was opening in Sienna and 80 was at the orchestrator's. However, his biggest contribution to the opera form came when he introduced instrumental accompaniment to the recitative in 1686, although his choice of bassoon and triangle is now regarded as misguided.

Throughout the first half of the eighteenth century, opera was largely engaged in fundraising, an aspect of the craft that has remained its central concern ever since. In London, George Frideric Handel wrote in the Italian *opera sera* style, a genre not known for having them exactly rolling in the aisles. Even so, a mid-career tribute show called *Handel This* was performed at Drury Lane in 1728, parodying Handel's most popular tunes and satirising the court of George II, particularly his parsimonious nature. Unfortunately, the King failed to see the funny side, demanded his money back and had the Gents Chorus hanged at Tyburn. The producers prudently cancelled the regional tour.

Handel specialised in penning extraordinary arias for the *castrati* and one would have thought they'd welcome some comic material, having little else to raise a laugh in their testicular-challenged lives. *Castrati* were venerated by the theatre audiences of the day, showered with gifts and welcomed into the fashionable salons. Their voices had the range of a woman supported by the power of a man and they also saved on dressing-rooms, being able to muck in with the sopranos without the threat of scandal. However, castration began to outweigh the lures of show-business and the chance to see sopranos undressing, and many years later the practice was abandoned, to be replaced by countertenors and the occasional lesbian with big lungs.

Meanwhile John Gay avoided royal censure but gained enormous box-office success with *The Beggar's Opera* in 1728. It wasn't strictly speaking an opera; he'd used popular tunes of the day as settings for his lyrics, passing it off as homage, the French word for 'rip-off'. *The Beggar's Opera* was a knock-about burlesque attacking the class system and government corruption, although purists would call it a piece of music theatre rather than a true opera—which certainly explains its excellent box-office returns. Gay attempted to capitalise on the success with a sequel entitled *The Beggar's Opera—the Early Years* but it failed to capture the public imagination and the backers lost their shirts. Their trousers were later sold to cover the backpay owing to the crew. However, Gay did go on to build the first opera theatre at Covent Garden in 1732. *The Times* ran the story 'Gay Opera Building Opens' on its front page, a reputation and headline the House has been trying to shake off ever since.

Across the Channel in Europe, Lully, Rameau, Keiser and Sergeant Schütz continued building an audience for opera with some really good work in the schools. Gluck's *Orfeo* of 1762 was groundbreaking, doing away with the traditional *da capo* aria, which had always held up the action through endless repetition. In the notorious Saturday matinee performance of Scarlatti's No. 78 (see above), the Site Inspector's aria had been repeated no less than sixteen times with a short dinnerbreak in between. But now there was a strong connection between the musical drama and the emotive power of the text, a nexus that Mozart was to exploit brilliantly in all his works. He mirrored society with wit and energy and his librettists shot their arrows at any number of targets. The fact that *The Magic Flute* made absolutely no sense to any rational person was interpreted by the critics as a withering attack on Austrian recreational drug use. *Cosi fan Tutte* could be seen as pre-feminist polemic or patriarchal diatribe depending on who was singing Despina. In *Don Giovanni*, Mozart crafts a central villian of enormous appeal despite his moral failings, although poor diction on opening night left the audience confused when it appeared that the Don was having it off with his manservant Leporello as well.

Opera buffa and *opera comique* emerged as two distinct styles. Neither was overly hilarious; *comique* actually implies that the work has spoken dialogue. Beethoven, known for his deadpan sense of humour and deft touch, wrote *Fidelio*, considered by many to be the greatest opera of them all and technically an *opera comique* even though you can count the laughs with your hands tied behind your back. He followed it up with a sequel called *Non-Fidelio*, a look at the lighter side of divorce. The opera was banned by papal edict and, fearing a backlash from the conservative Italian houses, Beethoven's agent persuaded him to withdraw it. Curiously, Italians had no problem with the moral ambiguities of Rossini, although their fiery Mediterranean temperaments always had a weakness for a crescendo that Rossini was happy to indulge. His comic operas were not inherently satirical; Verdi's covertly political works had greater social impact, but Rossini's operas remain popular partly because of their affectionate sending-up of human folly—*William Tell* is a hoot! Now here's a funny thing: at Rossini's funeral in Paris in 1868, the *Funeral March* by Beethoven was played on an ensemble of recently invented saxophones. Nothing to do with opera but I thought you might be interested.

Another German took the opera to new heights of hilarity:

Richard Wagner. Anyone who can expect an audience to sit through fourteen hours of music with a chromatic resolution every two hours if you're lucky has got to have a sense of humour. Little wonder that Wagner was a great favourite of that other happy-go-lucky German Adolf Hitler.

From the winning side of two future world wars came operas that succeeded because people remembered the tunes and recognised the characters. Offenbach disguised his attacks on the Second Empire under the veil of humour—the veil covering the female chorus line was much more transparent. Across the Channel, the quintessentially English pairing of W.S. Gilbert and A. Sullivan produced a body of work often held up as the pinnacle of satirical operetta, although their most subversive work is rumoured to be locked in a safe in the offices of D'Oyly Carte's solicitors. The story goes that it's a ribald attack on Victorian morals penned by Gilbert in a less guarded moment. Of course, what threatened to raise the hackles of staid Victorians would barely raise the jaded eyebrow of today's hardened eight-year-olds, so I daresay it could be safely added to the school curriculum.

The end of the nineteenth century saw opera manifesting itself in numerous guises: the seriousness of Wagner, Verdi and the realists like Puccini, the light-heartedness of the Viennese school or the vague social commentary of the fourteenth touring production of *HMS Pinafore*. Unfortunately, the First World War had a dampening effect on all of them. Apart from the fact that most of the eligible stage crew were wiped out in Flanders, the opera seemed ill-equipped to respond to the horrors of the Western Front. The artistic vacuum was filled by the avant-garde but the only Dadaist opera ever commissioned (for two pianos, a urinal and three baritone amputees) closed at its first rehearsal. Brecht and Weil wrote the bitter *Die Dreigroschen Oper* (or *The Two Cent Opera* in decimal currency) but even its bleak vision of the world underestimated the depths of human nature which would be plumbed by the Nazis scarcely a decade later. Alban Berg combined toe-tapping tunes and a jaunty plot for the laugh-a-minute *Lulu* while the Russians, never afraid of a good night out, filled the theatres with silly-season fare like *Lady Macbeth of Mtsensk*. In England, Benjamin Britten combined a love of chunky knitwear and atonalism in *Billy Budd* and *Peter Grimes* and throughout the latter half of the twentieth century, composers pursued experimentation in form and content. John Adams enjoyed success with *Nixon in China* but its companion piece *Nixon in the Bahamas* went nowhere. Phillip Glass abandoned serious music for a lucrative career writing ring tones for mobile phones.

So whither the opera as we move into the twenty-first century? New works are hard to come by, being expensive to produce, and opera companies now rely heavily on reinterpreting the classics. The rise in popularity of music theatre has proven competitive and a modern audience's thirst for realism makes it harder for those singers physically matched to opera's demands to look the part—one simply doesn't believe Mimi is dying of consumption when she's the size of a barn and looks like she ate the string section for lunch. Smaller, more intimate works reflecting contemporary concerns may prove the genre's saviour and I'm sure we all look forward to a chance to sit with ten other people, enthralled as we watch two anorexic singers chronicle a long and painful death from asbestosis, set to the discordant scratchings of a zither and looped electronic industrial noise. Especially at $123 plus booking fee!

AD 1891

The birth of the labour movement

In October, 1886, the Queensland town of Crackensak sweltered under a blinding sun that pushed the mercury to the highest temperature since record keeping began. As record keeping had only begun the week before, the event went largely unheralded, and out on the vast sheep stations the shearers went about their business with heads down and clippers flying, sending the dust motes swirling through the rays of a sun that had risen that morning at 6.12 and shone in the cloudless skies of a high pressure system with a relative humidity of 73 per cent.

Just out of town on Bringabirralong Station, Squatter Lewis ran four thousand head of sheep with the same grim determination that he brought to bear on his long-suffering family and any hapless individual who came looking for a job of work. The station foreman Bill Ryan had coined the nickname 'Nasty Lewis' for him, but it had never really stuck. Bill was a man of little imagination and that was the best he could come up with under pressure one night in the stockyard when the lads had been sharing an ale and a grumble about the boss.

Even now, several of the lads occasionally muttered 'Nasty Lewis' but it was more to make Bill feel better about himself than anything else.

Out in the sheds on that scorching day, the shearing crew had just finished their lunchtime tucker, a choice of damper and dripping or a light tuna salad tossed through with sesame oil and capers, when Squatter Lewis stormed in. 'Listen well, you lazy bastards!' he roared above the clatter of machinery and plaintive bleating of the ewes. 'Every man jack of you is going to double his quota by sunset or there'll be no work for you useless pissants on the morrow!'

'I'm terribly sorry—I didn't quite catch that last bit ...' said Cloth-ears Pete, a mild-mannered lanolin gatherer from County Corkbord. The squatter's stockwhip cracked with a well-aimed ferocity and Pete's bifocals flew from his face and went skittering across the floor. As he scrabbled blindly for them the squatter, snorting with laughter, ground the heel of his boot into Pete's lanolin-softened hand, which honestly looked a good fifteen years younger than the rest of him.

'Once more for the bog-Irish, is it?' sneered Lewis. 'Right. I want the rest of the flock shorn by sundown or there's nothing for you tomorrow. Plain enough?'

'But if we shear them all today there'll be no more work for us tomorrow regardless,' stammered one of the fleece-combers.

'Well, then,' said Lewis, temporarily at a loss. 'There'll be nothing for you next year either! And I'll personally make sure you never work in this agricultural district again!' And with that he turned and strode out into the heat and dust.

The men stood in a resentful silence broken only by a muttered 'Nasty Lewis!' once the squatter was well out of earshot. The ringer half-heartedly ordered them back to work.

'Ach, what's the point?' cried Dougal McGinty, a fiery Scot from Perthshire whose face was constantly peeling, despite a strict moisturising regimen. 'Why break our backs for the bosses? Aren't we worth a decent day's wages and a bit of respect? Ah sure, I'm not expecting him to know our first names or birthdays but a nod and a handshake wouldn't be going astray now, would it?'

There was a murmur of cautious approval.

'Don't we deserve better than this? It's time the working men of the Great South Land stood up to these two-bit tyrants!'

The murmur grew in enthusiasm, with shouts of 'Aye!' and 'Seems reasonable!' Dougal sensed a surging wave of support.

'I'm calling a meeting in the cockies' camp tonight!' he cried. 'Shall we say seven for seven-thirty?'

'Huzza!' roared the lads in lusty unison and they threw themselves at the sheep with renewed vigour, minds racing with tantalising visions of grassroots campaigning and placard design. And so it was on the dusty plains of Queensland that a powerful force for social change was born ...

Dougal McGinty shooed away the dog and mounted the tuckerbox himself, gazing at the men gathered before him in the flickering firelight. Honest working men, like Nugget Clark, Squinty Logan and Unkempt Warren. Cloth-ears Pete was there, patiently trying to repair his spectacles with plaited native grasses, while Bill Ryan searched his newly bought thesaurus for a better nickname. In the distance, Dougal could hear the plaintive cadence of little Jimmy Tamor's harmonica, floating on the still night air (4° above the average) all the way from the ablutions block where Jimmy had to go to practice because the lads couldn't stand it any longer. Didn't these men deserve a decent day's pay for a decent day's labour and some sort of manageable framework for workplace behavioural practices?

'Lads,' he began in his thick brogue, 'the time has come for us to join together—for ourselves and for the sake of our children. United we stand, divided we fall. Sons of the South, awake, arise! The time has come to gather together and form ... a union!'

The silence was deafening.

McGinty looked around, bewildered. 'Well, you all seemed pretty keen this afternoon. Will no-one join with me now to throw the bosses from our backs?'

Squinty Logan looked down and poked the ground with the toe of his boot. 'Well, Dougal, to be perfectly honest—and I think I'm speaking for the boys here—I have a lot of trouble with the word "union". Am I right, lads?'

There were murmurs of agreement.

'Okay, sure, let's work towards some sort of relationship structure with management but we have to find new ways to facilitate that agenda other than the conflict models of the past. I mean, it's not us and them.'

McGinty couldn't believe his ears. 'Yes it is,' he said incredulously. 'It's exactly us and bloody them! They live in mansions and dine off bone china while we eat the scraps from their table and swelter in this shitheap!'

'I think "shitheap" is the kind of intemperate language we should be avoiding. And I think the bunkhouse looks a lot nicer since Nugget did the Roman blinds ...'

'And Cookie's done a great job with the menu,' added Nugget.

'Alright, yes, the blinds are good,' said McGinty exasperatedly. 'And yes, Salad Thursday was a marvellous innovation but our children trudge miles to a clapped-out schoolhouse while the boss's spawn ride to private colleges in broughams and landaus! How much more us and them do you want?'

'Sure, there are inequality issues—and I take your point about the transport options—but you have to look at it from a broader perspective. Our employment opportunities only come through their entrepreneurial utilisation of capital,' offered Bow-legged Bruce, as the other men nodded in agreement.

'And their capital only comes from our sweat and blood! Didn't any of you read the tracts I left in the latrine?'

'Oh. Were they there for reading?' asked Unkempt Warren guiltily.

'Alright,' said Dougal. 'Answer me this: what would Squatter Lewis be doing without us? How many sheep would he be shearing with his manicure set, or Mrs Lewis with her pinking shears, before the footrot set in and every man jack merino's arse was flyblown?'

'Er … nine, maybe ten?' offered Unkempt Warren.

'None, you idiot! Sure, we need his wages but by Jesus he'd not have the shirt on his back without us.'

'Fine, it's a two-way street, Dougal. But we're all pulling in the one direction,' said Nugget, somewhat confusingly. 'As an aspirational voter …'

'Perspirational, more like,' muttered an increasingly frustrated McGinty under his breath.

'And that's exactly the kind of old-school personal denigration we can do without in today's workplace,' admonished Squinty Logan. 'Your point, Nugget?'

'I just can't see the benefit of a union. I feel I can negotiate my own career outcomes more successfully as an individual in an enterprise-bargaining situation.'

McGinty laughed out loud. 'Oh really? When was the last time you sat down in Lewis' drawing room and chatted about the roster?'

'Well, we haven't been able to match up our diaries just yet …' said Nugget feebly.

'And you never will! Don't you see, lads? A union would give us power! Think what'd happen if every shearer in Australia downed tools and said, "No more! Treat us with the respect we deserve!" '

'We'd have the mums and dads offside for a start. No-one likes to be inconvenienced.'

'We *are* the mums and dads! Well, we're the dads—and don't start on about the tragically childless,' said Dougal with a warning look as Squinty opened his mouth to speak. 'I tell you, a man on his own is just that, but when people get together ... they can give each other the courage to dance through fire.'

Bow-legged Bruce shrugged his shoulders and threw the dregs of his tea on the embers. 'It's not the fire I'm worried about, Dougal. It's the getting fired that bothers me.'

'And I'm sure Mr Lewis gives a lot to charity; you know, anonymously like,' said Squinty quickly.

'Right—that's it!' seethed McGinty, clambering down. 'Why waste my time with you lily-livered running dogs? You can sort out your bloody class divide yourselves!'

The men turned to each with raised eyebrows as he stormed out of the camp in a huff. 'Well,' said Nugget laconically. 'That kind of behaviour might go down well in the gulag but it's hardly the attitude we need to get ahead in this country. What say we form the Australian Labor Party instead?'

Show me the Monet

Spring had come early to the village of Giverny and throughout its Norman streets, dotted in the window boxes and the neatly tilled garden beds, perennials quivered towards the sun, annuals did likewise, and deciduous trees sent forth budding leaves with the delicate precision of a Yates catalogue. And nowhere was this shyly exuberant reawakening more exquisitely displayed than in the garden of Claude Monet.

Taking a promenade before breakfast, Monet sniffed the air, feeling in Nature's affirmation his own creative juices beginning to flow with renewed vigour. It's either that or dyspepsia, he thought, walking to the potting shed to issue instructions to the gardeners who tended his living palette. Its construction had been quite an immense effort—forty-four part-time jobs created and a sizeable economic knock-on effect, as the town mayor proudly told anyone who would listen. The waterlily pond had been dug out by hand in the face of feverish opposition from his ill-informed neighbours who feared his exotic plants, and an arm of the River Ept was diverted to avoid the Stage Two water restrictions. A Japanese bridge had been artfully installed, although in all truth it was no more Japanese than Claude, having been built to order by an ornamental garden bridge manufactury in Lyons.

With a final glance and a nod of satisfaction, Monet turned and strode up the gravel path to the drawing room where his wife was taking breakfast.

'Good morning, dear Alice. Today I am going to paint waterlilies.'

'Is that such a good idea?' asked Alice, barely raising her eyes from the newspaper. 'We've got waterlilies coming out of our ears. They're not moving as well in the shop as they used to.'

Monet's balloon of self-content was swiftly punctured. Briskly unfolding his napkin and moving to the buffet, he grumbled: 'Who cares about the gift shop? I'm an artist, not a salesman! I quest to understand the elusive qualities of light, to transmogrify the ephemeral ...'

'Something's got to pay for the paint,' said Mme Monet before her husband could get up a head of steam. 'Couldn't you do a few more green Chinese women? They sold like hot cakes. Or turn out two dozen sad clowns, they were virtually walking out the door. Oh, and don't forget your BAS is due in tomorrow.'

Claude groaned. His last business activity statement had taken him three weeks to complete—he'd knocked off twenty studies of Rouen Cathedral in half that time. It was both ridiculous and demeaning. How could he, an artist of the first order, a friend of Clemençeau, Rodin and Manet, be expected to calculate one-eleventh of the depreciation on the cost price of a green wooden bridge? And if he crossed it without his easel, did that count as personal use? His last accountant had been all but useless. He still shuddered to think of his tax audit and the commissioner's refusal to allow absinthe as a tool of trade.

How did they think he saw those colours? By accident?

'Petty bureaucrats,' he muttered, raising a tureen lid. 'Oh brilliant! Still no devilled kidneys! Can anyone give me any medical evidence to support this wretched diet? Stupid doctor wouldn't know his arse from his elbow.'

'Stop muttering, dear. If you've got problems, talk to van Gogh, he'll lend an ear.' Mme Monet barked with laughter. In her youth she had dreamt of a career on the variety stage but had never pursued the profession; Claude sometimes wished she had. Carrying his *bran des sultanes* with skim milk to the table, he sat down dejectedly, only to be disturbed by a knock at the door.

A young woman stood on the step. 'Bonjour, my name is Brittany,?' she said brightly. 'I was wondering if you'd considered switching to one of the new postal companies? We have some great plans? Like, thirty centimes for the first eighteen items carried up to 1.6 kilometres, thirty-two thereafter or a flat forty centimes for friends and family on our *Bon Copains* Plan provided you post your letters between the hours of 6 and 9p.m.?'

'It is half past bloody eight in the morning,' said Claude testily. 'Don't you people have anything better to do?'

The girl studied her product notes in confusion. She was only doing this job because it beat seasonal fruit picking. Training had been nominal, and paint-spattered eccentrics wearing smocks had not been mentioned at the sales briefing.

'What the hell was wrong with the nationalised postal service anyway? I gave them the letter, they carried it in a bag then gave it to someone else—it's not as if it's hot-air balloon science! Hardly needs the cutting innovation of a thrusting free market, does it?'

'Er ... we have different coloured stamps ...' piped Brittany hopefully as the door slammed in her face.

'Why do people waste so much time on mundanities, trying to save half a sou on a postcard, for God's sake!' thundered Claude as he returned to his soggy breakfast. 'I'll tell you why—because some idiotic politician thinks cutting two francs off the price of a bale of hay for your horse will win him some votes. Freedom of choice is no freedom at all, it merely chokes your mind with the inconsequential, distracts you from the truth. No wonder the country's going to *les chiens*!'

Mme Monet stayed silent. Her husband cursing in English was always a sign of a stormy day ahead. No sooner had he raised his decaffeinated coffee to his lips than there came another knock at the door.

'Pretend you're not here,' she said as her husband began to melt with indignation. 'Or pretend you're someone else—Madame Curie shouldn't be too hard, seeing you're an impressionist.' Mme Monet made a choking noise and doubled up with mirth at her own wit as Claude's *bran des sultanes* sailed harmlessly over her head, landing with a wet thud on a picture of haystacks covering a crack in the wall.

This time it was a young man standing on the step, collection tin in hand with an indecipherable identity badge pinned to his shapeless chemise. 'Bonjour, man, I was like wondering if you'd care to give something to homeless youth?'

'Yes—diphtheria,' said Claude, slamming the door with a vigour that rattled the glassware. Ignoring his doctor's orders, he stormed over to the buffet and piled a plate high with bacon, not even bothering to avoid the fatty rashers. 'I tell you, Alice, it's becoming bloody impossible to be a creative genius these days! Nothing but constant distractions. I bet Bach didn't have to put up with this.'

'He had twenty children.'

'Ten francs says he didn't have to change their nappies, join the P&C and spend weekends on retreat getting in touch with his inner sense of fatherhood. No, he got to write cantatas and play the organ all day in peace.'

'Sounds like Mrs Bach got her fair share of his organ as well!' said Mme Monet before turning red and keeling over in hysterics.

With a sigh, Monet summoned the maid who promptly appeared and administered the Heimlich manoeuvre to the recumbent mistress of the house. Having restored a regular breathing pattern, she bobbed a curtsy and began to clear the breakfast dishes.

'Begging your pardon, sir, but cook was wondering if you'd given any thought to her allocated day off.'

'I beg your pardon?'

'Staff roster, sir. And Monsieur Jeevres was enquiring after allocated superannuation funds, now that the employer contribution's gone up to nine per cent …' she trailed off, as her master went the colour of the façade of Rouen Cathedral at sunset. Grabbing the *plongeur de café*, she turned and fled. Minutes later, a trembling hand edged through the doorway holding the morning's post. Monet snatched it from her and tore open a letter from the prefecture of Paris.

'Dear M. Monet,' it read. 'It is with deep regret that I must tell you the board of governors has rejected your application for the post of civic muralist. After a lengthy consultation process with aldermen, alderwomen and all de other people, it has been decided that your *style impressioniste* is a little too modern for our tastes and we have opted for a portaitist of the realism school, one who can paint eyes that really follow you around the *salle*. However, should you wish, you may lodge an appeal against this decision with the Tribunal of Equal Employment Opportunities within twenty-eight days at a fee of two francs. We remain respectfully yours …'

Monet crumpled the letter and threw it into the teapot.

'Right, that's it, I give up. If you'll excuse me, my dear, I shall retire to the studio to paint twenty studies of a green Chinese woman sitting in dappled sunlight from dawn to dusk. In the immortal words of Horace: if you can't beat 'em, coin 'em.'

AD 1903

The Wright stuff

Wilbur Wright was born in New Castle, Indiana, on 16 April 1867. His twin brother Orville was born four years later in Dayton, Ohio, where the family had moved when Momma got too plain tired of waiting for him to make an appearance. Orville entered this world on 19 August 1871, the fourth son of a preacher man, Daddy being a bishop of the United Brethren church, simple folk who knew their place in God's kingdom and gave thanks to the Creator every day for his divine mercy.

The Wright Girls, or the Wright Boys as neighbourhood folks got to calling them more correctly once they'd had their hair cut short and grew tired of wearing skirts, were easygoing fellas. Their schooling was nothing so's you'd notice—being in the service of the Lord, Daddy moved about a lot and they never graduated from high school but, boy, could they turn their hands to anything of a mechanical persuasion. Always a'tinkerin' with toys and such that they made theirselves in the poky shed down the bottom of Bishop Wright's yard, and selling them for a nickel from a little old stall they set up on the sidewalk. But they was canny with it—the wind-up key cost you a dollar and a half. You take a poke round your attic and see if you got one gathering dust, gosh, a Wright brothers toy'd fetch you a fortune these days, it'd be the best nickel you ever spent! But that was then and this is now, and tomorrow—well, that's just a maybe and the day after that don't bear thinking about.

Any old how, gizmos and gadgets just started eating up more and more of their lives. They didn't have no time for soirees or picnics and they wasn't that interested in the lady folks. Not that they was funny that way—heck, no! Bishop Wright woulda put a stop to that double quick, the United Brethren not standin' for any of your same-sex behaviour unless you was a qualified member of the clergy. It was just that while a well-turned ankle or a glitter in the eye mighta made the boys snap to and notice, there was always a double-cam crankshaft or a new pair of pliers waiting around the corner to set their attention on the fairer sex a'wavering.

Round about 1891, the Wright brothers set up a bicycle shop, renting and selling the newfangled machines to just about anybody who could stump up the deposit. Pretty soon they started tinkerin' away and makin' their own improvements, so no-one was surprised when they set to manufacturing the velocipedes theirselves, working out of a first-floor factory above the store. You take a poke round your attic and see if you got a Wright brothers bike gathering dust, gosh, it'd fetch you a fortune! But that was then etc. and so on.

Still, bicycles weren't the be-all and end-all and for no apparent reason, Wilbur got to thinking about heavier-than-air flying machines and soon developed quite a passion for the science of aer-o-planes. Only trouble was, there weren't no such things about at the time, and he got to moping, it being kinda difficult to have a hobby that nobody had invented yet. So one day in the bicycle workshop, he put down the bell he was a'tinkerin' with and unburdened hisself to his brother.

'Orville,' said he, 'I've been thinkin' that maybe we should start a line in heavier-than-air flying machines.'

'But we sell bicycles, Wilbur. I can't see how we're goin' to move many aer-o-planes when a customer comes lookin' for something of the two-wheeled, self-propelled earthbound variety. Besides, as far as I'm aware, no reliable manufacturer has got on top of the problem of sustained mechanical flight. Where we gonna get the supplier?'

'Well, you know we like a'tinkerin' … I was kinda wondering if we could do it ourselves.'

'Heck—why not? We could close the store on Saturdays, it's not like there's the demand for six-day bicycle retail. But maybe we should ask Daddy if this is going to be okay with the Church.'

'I don't know about that, the Church has always got an objection to something,' said Wilbur, closing the blinds in case someone out on the street could lip-read. 'Let's keep this under our hats, little brother.'

And so they did, hidin' their preparatory sketches under their hats and building a wind tunnel, and if nosy folks asked what the heck it was for, Orville'd say they was testing streamlined handlebars or some such. Ev'ry Saturday morning they'd repair to Perkins' old grain store, which they'd turned into a kinda rudimentary aeronautics laboratory, starting from scratch 'cos you couldn't get the plans from nowhere, and calibrate their tables of lift and air pressure over a curved flyin' surface. By the fall of that year, eighteen hundred and somethin', they had a little model, made up of old pieces of packin' crate and the rear frame of a 26" Ladies Tourer, liftin' off the ground when they cranked the fan up to high speed. Wilbur came over all excited and had to go for a lie-down, reading Paul's Letters to the Corinthians to calm his fevered mind. Poor guy had been a martyr to his funny turns ever since he got hit in the face with a baseball bat when he was a kid. Didn't do his teeth much good, neither.

By 1902 they'd done built a glider and, after taking it apart into bits they could fit inside the saddle-bags on their bicycles, they transported the whole kit and caboodle to Kitty Hawk in North Carolina. Out there on the sandy dunes, they put it back together, though Orville got in a jam when he put Tab A into Slot B on the tail section, knowin' full well in retrospect that the pesky thing shoulda gone into Slot C and no amount of hammerin' was gonna make a difference. But learners make mistakes and within two days, their machine was ready for flyin'. Not that this was your self-propelled aer-o-plane, no, sir. You still had to run down a hill or pull hard on a long piece of string but the boys got to learn how to fly it, strapping theirselves to the frame and taking off in little hops before easin' back down to earth, though truth be told, Wilbur come down one time a little on the heavy side and twisted his ankle, it was swollen up like a football and everythin'. Couldn't get in the air for a fortnight and Orville had to dink him back into town every afternoon when it got too dark for flyin'.

O'course the bicycle sales took a dive 'cos the boys had their minds on other things, but now they'd figured out a wing warp system to keep the machine in the air. Or so they said; the whole thing was way over my head, bein' nothin' but a nipper at the time. Next step was to nut out a way to strap an engine on to get the thing movin' of its own accord. Keepin' the weight down was the important thing, and that weren't helped by Wilbur bein' a little on the chubby side, havin' as he did a liking for cream horns and deep-fryin'. So Wilbur decided to swallow his pride and go on the Weight Watchers program and Orville went along to the meetin's to keep him company, it bein' that much easier to reach your weight loss goal with a fat-fightin' buddy by your side. And as an added bonus, losing a few pounds gave them both a lot more energy and the five servings of vegetables a day kept 'em cleaner on the inside.

They got to designing a gasoline engine that was light as a feather with a whole mess of metal glued to it but even with a new-look, slimline Wilbur sitting at the controls, they just couldn't get the lift they needed. So they sat and scratched their heads for a coupla days, munching on fat-free yoghurt until Orville had a brainwave. He suddenly turned to his brother and said: 'Why don't we just go bi?'

Well, Wilbur sat there and blinked hard, not quite sure what Orville was getting at and a little afraid to ask.

'Two wings instead of one,' explained Orville, putting his arms atop o' each other to demonstrate.

Wilbur let out a sigh of relief—he hadn't known how he was goin' to break the bi news to their Daddy—and straight-aways started doodlin' some sketches of the proposed wing configuration while mentally calculating the additional weight of the extra aerofoil and the bracin' wire. Heck, he'd have to go down to seventeen points a day just to make up for it! And o' course, they'd have to make twice as many trips to Kitty Hawk to transport the thing in their saddle-bags, but the Lord moves in mysterious ways: exercise is a weight-watcher's best friend.

And so it was on 17 December 1903, with only eight shopping days to go till Christmas including that one, that the Wright brothers tightened the last nut on their flying machine and hauled the strange-lookin' beast into place on its sixty-foot launching rail. They'd named it *The Flyer* — okay, not all that imaginative but they were bicycle salesmen after all—and she stood forty and one half feet across the wings, powered by a twelve horsepower engine which made one hell of a din. After a final weigh-in, Wilbur started cussin' that doughnut he hadn't been able to resist at mornin' tea and Orville got the nod as first pilot. He strapped on his knee-pads and goggles and climbed into the harness, sitting next to the gas donkey that drove two propellers behind the wings. They was just goin' to fire her up when a short little man carryin' a clipboard came a'running towards them, arms waving about like a windmill.

'Hey, you there!' he shouted. 'This is limited airspace! You two cowboys filed a flight plan?'

Orville looked at Wilbur in amazement. 'We're plannin' on being the first people to fly anywheres—that's about the only plan we got,' he said, trying to keep a polite tone in his voice like Daddy woulda wanted.

'Don't mean you can ignore the regulations. This crate airworthy?'

'That's what we're here to try and find out,' said Wilbur.

'Well, you got to sign an indemnity form. As the statutory authority controlling the Kitty Hawk sand dunes, we can't afford to have you fly-boys breakin' a leg and then hollerin' to some judge on the county circuit like it was all our fault. You carrying any sharp metallic objects? Nail scissors or the like? You imbibed any intoxicating liquors in the last twenty-four hours? And, hey, wait a minute,' said the little man, eyes suddenly narrowing, 'what are your names?'

'Wilbur and Orville Wright.'

'Hmm. Well, that don't sound too Arabian. Okay, you got clearance but it's going to cost you twenty-four bucks.'

Wilbur started on mutterin' as he opened his pocket-book and paid the man but finally they was ready, 'xcept Orville couldn't find the keys to the engine, so there was a bit o' fussin' about that until he remembered they was in his pocket all the time. She fired perfect first-up, the props started spinnin' like a dervish and it were as if we was in a sand storm in the desert.

Then *The Flyer* kind o' shuddered and started movin' down the launch rail, gatherin' speed until she was up, up—musta been ten, twenty feet off the ground and flying along at near on thirty mile an hour. Wilbur let out a mighty whoop and we started runnin' down the sand after her, chasin' history as she sputtered along, yawin' and ptichin' a little ways but Orville had her under control, no doubt about it. Twelve seconds later she come down to earth, gentle as a lamb, like she were wore out after flying all of one hundred and twenty feet.

The brothers just hugged each other like there were no-one watching, slapping each other's backs, tears near streamin' down their faces! I didn't wanna be the Afr'can Amer'can in the woodpile and point out that they'd only gone one hundred and twenty feet and if they was gonna try and fly to the state capital that'd be a awful lot of hops, 'specially as they had to move the launch rail forward one hundred and twenty feet every time. No, I let them have the moment, standin' in front of the photographer, though I'd a thought there'd be more press fellas there, somethin' like the *Church News* at least. It were quite a low-key affair and straightaways we were all a-haulin' *The Flyer* back up the dunes for another attempt to break the world record for heavier-than-air flight. Shouldn't be hard, I thought to myself, only got to beat twelve seconds.

And right enough, they flew all day, Wilbur comin' out on top with a flight 852 feet long in just shy of a minute. Orville chiacked him straight up, sayin' if *The Flyer* could carry Mr Tubby that far, she could carry anythin', and Wilbur looked kinda hurt, 'cos doughnut aside, he thought he'd managed to take control of his dietin' destiny. But then we was all distracted by a fella watchin' us from the dunes, dressed up in some kinda dog suit, with a bevy o' ladies from the local burlesque house hangin' off his arms. The photographer skedaddled off to take a picture of him right there and then and when they was finished with that, the fella wandered over.

'Well, hello there,' he said, takin' off the pooch head and speakin' like a Limey.

'Afternoon,' said Wilbur, tentative like.

'I've been watching your flying machine. Quite the thing, what? Tell me—how many passengers can she take?'

'Well, sir,' said Orville slowly. 'We're still in the prototype phase, she just carries the pilot. But if we can elevate the lift-to-thrust ratio, I guess she could take just about anything.'

'Best we leave that technical mumbo jumbo to you back-room johnnies,' said the Englishman, who hadn't got round to saying just who he was. He was lookin' real hard at *The Flyer*, walkin' around and kickin' the skids.

'We?' said Wilbur, kinda puzzled.

'Well, you chaps can sell the science but you need someone who can sell the potential. You think people are going to take the train to the coast when they can fly there? Honeymooning in Niagara? Fly there faster and have more time in the barrel! I know this stuff. Tell me, how far down the track are you with prioritising heavy traffic routing? Have you got a paperless ticketing system in mind? Discount fare structures, non-unionised labour, a work force in touch with today's young-sters—no offence, but you're both getting on a bit and you're a little on the hefty side. Last thing travellers want to see when they step on board.'

Wilbur gritted his teeth, rememb'ring his Daddy's words about kindness to strangers. 'No offence taken.'

'It's all about publicity, you see, making an impact in the market. You've got the product but where are the press? You've managed one chap with a Box Brownie whereas I can put you on every front page from New York to San Francisco.

'And why would we want that, mister?' said Orville.

'To sell tickets! This industry's all about volume: punters in, punters off, profits up! Do you do inflight catering?'

'No, sir.'

'That's a plus. Total waste of money to give the stuff away—value-add by selling on board. Any entertainment—distributing playing cards, phonograph, pinochle, that sort of thing?'

'Heck no—we only got the thing in the air this morning,' said Orville, wiltin' under the Limey's relentless enthusiasm.

'The time to start making a fortune is yesterday. Enterpreneurs get in on the ground floor.'

Then just as our new best friend was 'bout to take a breath, blow me down if we didn't have another visitor. Military guy by the looks, proddin' the wing fabric and twangin' the bracin' wires.

'Can I help you?' said Wilbur, losin' patience with all the nosy parkers.

'Where do you put the guns on this thing?'

'Beggin' your pardon, sir, but what in God's name would we be wantin' with a gun on a flying machine?'

'Think about it, son,' said the army man. 'Ten of these babies comin' in low over the horizon, Gatling gun blazin' on each wing. Don't reckon your enemy'd stand much of a chance, huh?'

'Now hang on a cotton-pickin' minute, we never built this machine to do no harm to anybody,' said Wilbur, all testy.

'Don't you know there's a war on?' fired back the stranger.

'No, sir, I was not aware of that.'

'Well, there's bound to be one on somewhere. You got something against America, boy?'

'I'm as patriotic as the next man but that ain't the way our Daddy brought us up.'

'What, he a red of some kind?'

'No, sir, he's a Bishop of the United Brethren.'

'Then he'd know that God is on the side of the big battalions and with a squadron of these mothers kickin' ass I don't reckon a battalion'd come much bigger.'

The Wright brothers looked at each other in confusion. Things were way outta hand and their blood sugar was gettin' low. And then to make matters worse, an old geezer hove into view, a-hollerin' and cussin'.

'Which of you idiots been flying that thing? I represent the Kitty Hawk Residents' Association and you can't come in here makin' that God-awful racket! You done put my chickens off layin'!'

'Back off, mister,' snarled the military man. 'This is henceforth a restricted military zone and under Section 42C of the Proud American Act of 1903 I can have you incarcerated if you do not desist at once.'

Well, that stopped the old coot right in his tracks. Meanwhile, the Limey in the dog suit started scratchin' something on a business card and handed it to Wilbur.

'That's my telephone number or you can wire me on the telegraph. Keep the dream alive. Now if you'll excuse me, I have to go and walk across the Grand Canyon on a tightrope. Fantastic publicity!'

And with that, he gathered up the showgirls and the mutt head then took off in a fancy motor car, horn goin' thirteen to the dozen, scatterin' promotional brochures like a ticker-tape parade down Main Street. Orville took his brother to one side.

'Listen, Wilbur, let's not be too hasty here. Now I know we never meant for this flyin' machine to be used for war, or for packin' in Joe Average like a sardine in a tin can to take him places he never really wanted to go to in the first place, but we gotta think of tomorrow. Somehow I don't think the future's in bicycles. If we play our cards right, big brother, we could clean up!'

Wilbur stared at the ground, kickin' up the sand in little puffs and thinkin'.

'Could I increase my daily carbohydrate intake?' he asked, hesitatin'.

'Absolutely. Heck, we'd never have to fly one of these things again if we didn't want to. As long as we find a good attorney to negotiate the intellectual property rights, why, you could blow out to the size of a barn and be none the poorer!'

And so, as the sun went down over the dunes o' Kitty Hawk, the Wright brothers marched into folklore, not to mention some fat juicy contracts with the military and the low-end high-volume travel industry. And the rest, as they say, is history. So go take a poke round your attic, 'cos boy, if you got one of the original Wright *Flyers* gathering dust up there, gosh, you got yourself a fortune!

Mind you, if you got an attic big enough to hold it, maybe you got yourself a fortune in the first place. And I'd be mighty happy to take it off your hands 'cos I'm the only sucker in this story who didn't make shit. Beggin' your pardon, Bishop.

News from the
front line

A long way from Tipperary, in the dull and bloodied winter of 1916, Private Peter Wardell sprinted across the cordite-shattered wastes of no-man's-land, ducking and weaving to avoid the shells and machine-gun fire slicing the air in a furious attempt to end his short and grubby life. Just like dodging the rozzers in Bendigo, apart from the machine guns, the shells and the shattered wastes, he thought, before abandoning the metaphor as hopelessly inadequate. He wasn't so much afraid as annoyed. While quietly minding his own business in a slit trench ahead of the line of the enemy barrage, Captain Wilkins, manning the only telephone line not cut to ribbons, had received a communique from HQ and passed it on for Private Wardell to deliver to the rear in wireless mode, or 'running' as the non-commissioned ranks knew it.

'Better be bloody important,' he now muttered to himself, leaping over the splayed corpse of a gunner, 'something worth getting my arse shot off for because I've grown quite attached to it.' As indeed he had, being attached to his arse ever since he was born in a tent on what little remained of the Victorian goldfields, his father having missed the gold rush by a good thirty years but remaining confident. Young Wardell had been running for much of his life, up before the magistrate for petty thieving (two apples and a lady's bonnet, non-related charges) and the army had offered a way out of his troubles. 'Out of the frying pan and into the fire,' he chortled, anticipating the unheard narrative thread before diving into the protection of the rearguard trench. Straightening his helmet and unbuttoning his tunic, he pulled from his pocket the vital slip of paper and, ducking his head under the sandbagged lintel, entered the command post of Major Looke.

'Message from HQ, sir, cc'ed from Captain Wilkins.'

'Thank you, private. The Bosch are laying it on thick this morning, what?' said Major Looke, opening the message to read it.

'My guess is they're laying down an offensive barrage, sir, to soften this already-weakened section of our forward line to try for an outflanking manoeuvre against the vulnerable rear,' said Private Wardell.

'Splendid, splendid,' said Major Looke, indulging his habit of ignoring anyone under the rank of sergeant and concentrating instead on the news from his superiors. Colonials, such as Wardell, had to wait for promotion to brigadier before Looke would even deign to look them in the eye, although he had a soft spot for Canadians, having always secretly admired the Mounted Police.

'I say, the War Office is sending us a squad of newspaper johnnies,' he informed his fellow officers, 'what's the phrase they use—ah, here it is: "embedded journalists", who can observe how the war's getting on, show the home front just how well we're doing, that sort of thing. Sounds a bit of fun. I daresay the old *paters familia* would be tickled pink as he tackles the morning kippers to see Looke Minor grinning up from the front page of *The Times*, what? Says here we're to organise a transport detail to pick them up at 15:00 hours. Bother, what's that in real time?'

'Er … four o'clock isn't it?' offered Captain Dilley.

'Three, sir,' said Wardell, politely.

'Really?' said Dilley. 'Ah … yes, of course, you take away twelve, don't you? Well, that explains the mix-up with yesterday's counterattack. Speaking of same, how are you going with those letters of condolence, Simpkin?'

'All done, sir, ready to post but I'm one stamp short.'

'And we'd best sharpen up, lads,' said the Major. 'Looks like Mrs Pankhurst has been at it again so there'll be one or two of the fairer sex amongst the Fleet Street scribes.'

'Permission to volunteer for transport detail and postoffice run, sir!' said Wardell, snapping smartly to attention.

'Permission granted, private. And see if you can rustle up a bit of the old war paint, could you? Wouldn't do any harm to look one's best for the photographs and I've been told by a sick friend that a pinch of rouge works wonders.'

At precisely 15:00 hours, Wardell drew up in the old Bedford outside the Hotel de Quatre Saisons in the relatively unscathed village of Chantillylace, three miles behind the line. Waiting in the lobby were a scruffy band of journalists trying to reconcile their expense accounts while arguing with the manager about his failure to open the bar.

'Yes, mate,' said one red-faced gent in a loud voice, talking slowly for the benefit of the non-English speaker, 'I do know there's a war on—didn't you read my piece for the *Mirror*? How could you miss the headline? It took up half the front page: "RUN! HUN! RUN!". Main feature below, ran for five pars.'

'Excuse me,' said a severe-looking woman in a daringly

short skirt that revealed her delicate kid-leather ankle boots. 'I paid for a room *avec bain* and there was *pas de bain* to be seen. I hope you realise that if I give this place a less-than-favourable review as a weekend getaway, you might as well send half the staff home now. Permanently!'

Private Wardell blew his whistle sharply and called the rabble to order.

'Pardon me, ladies and gents, but if you'll kindly walk this way, transport's arrived to take you up the front,' he said with a lewd wink to a young girl clutching a notebook and a cab-charge voucher.

The sight of the Bedford provoked a cry of horror from the travel correspondent for the *Telegraph*. 'You cannot be serious! Where are the taxis?'

'Major Looke's personal limousine,' grinned Wardell. 'Hang on tight because what's left of the road can be a bit bumpy,' he added before jumping into the cab and taking off with a sickening lurch. By the time they arrived at Looke's HQ, half the contingent were as green as the dead horse they'd stopped beside while waiting for a lull in the enemy bombardment to make the final dash to safety. The Major emerged from his bunker to welcome them.

'Jolly glad you could all make it,' he enthused, vigorously pumping hands. 'Probably best we all get inside, the Hun are putting on a few fireworks for your arrival, what?' As a shell exploded nearby, a strangulated scream came from the parapet and a newly severed left arm landed with a thud in front of the severe-looking woman, spraying her skirt with blood. 'You see?' said Looke nervously, ushering them into the dugout quickly to avoid an awkward PR situation. 'Everyone wants to shake hands!'

Crammed inside by the light of a guttering candle as the shells thumped monotonously into the earth above them sending cascades of dust spiralling through the fetid air, the Major gave his first press conference, Captain Dilley at his side to remind him of the protocols set out by the Home Department for dealing with the fourth estate. No-one had asked Private Wardell to leave so he stayed, unobserved in a dark corner of the shelter, hoping to catch another glimpse of an ankle.

'Well, good evening, ladies and gentlemen, and welcome to …'

Captain Dilley tugged urgently at Looke's sleeve and gave a quick shake of the head.

'Ah … I'm afraid I can't tell you exactly where we are, military secrets and what have you. I can tell you we're in France—I can even narrow that down and say northern France and we're currently fighting—can I tell them who we're fighting?'

Dilley consulted the Home Department manual then nodded.

'We're fighting the Germans, or as we know him here in the front line, Fritz, the Bosch, filthy Hun or Grinning Stümpfelpeiter. Actually that last one is a nickname I came up with but it doesn't seem to have caught on. Ne'er no mind. Now I've heard a lot of doomsayers rabbiting on about a stalemate on the Western Front that's going to drag on for years but in all fairness to the War Office, when they said it was going to be over by Christmas, they never actually said which one. Personally, I think we'll have it pretty much wrapped up by the August Bank Holiday but that's just my opinion and you can quote me on it. My name's Lord Kitchener.'

Looke's feeble attempt at humour was met with blank looks. A small ferrety man raised his hand.

'Murdoch, *Sun* newspaper. Kitchener—how do you spell that?'

'That was a joke.'

'Whole bleedin' thing's a joke,' snarled the representative from the *Workers' Daily*. 'This war is nothin' but the last gasp of imperialism and it's the workin' man who's bein' fed screamin' into the bloodstained mouths of the military industrial complex.'

'Er, quite,' said Looke. 'I suggest we keep question time until the end of the briefing, if you don't mind.'

'Just a quick one, sir,' interjected a reasonable looking chap from the *Globe*. 'Last November Scotland Yard raided the offices of my newspaper and destroyed the day's issue because we were critical of Lord Kitchener—not you, sir, the real one.' There were a few laughs from the better-informed among them. 'Does today's media access to the war situation herald a new era of openness from the military authorities?'

Looke turned pleadingly to Captain Dilley, who merely shrugged and thumbed through the index.

'Well, the army's never had anything to hide and we want to make sure that our loved ones at home know exactly what's going on, that they know that the Hun rape nuns on a daily basis and eat babies and so on.'

'And are you going to show us Huns eating babies?'

'Er, no—they tend to eat them in Belgium and that's proving rather difficult to get to. No, we'll be showing you daily life in the trenches—in fact, those interested can go out with the men on a night patrol to collect the dying this evening. I'll just need you to sign these indemnity forms and jot down your next of kin.'

There weren't any takers. The young lady Private Wardell had been secretly admiring raised her hand. 'Harriet Warrington-Smythe, *Dolly* Magazine. I've already noticed the awful hygienic conditions you live in and I'm sure my readers would be interested to know what sort of skin-care regimes you Tommies use to keep your faces feeling supple and battle-ready.'

'Ah—that one I can answer,' said Major Looke. 'I prefer a water-based moisturiser after a lemon scrub, particularly following a gas attack, which really clogs the pores ...'

Captain Dilley cleared his throat noisily and Looke tailed off.

'Andy McBride from *Inside Soccer*,' said a red-headed Scotsman rising laboriously to his feet, stomach reluctantly following. 'Following on from the success of the Christmas cease-fire football match, I was just wondering if Allied High Command have got any plans to shift talented midfielder Johnny Dumfries into a more attacking role for this year's friendly with the Germans, and secondly, if there's any realistic possibility of finding a decent playing surface in no-man's-land after the planned Somme offensive.'

'The first part of your question, I'll tackle that first—no pun intended.' And no pun taken, to judge from the stony silence. 'Um, sadly, Private Dumfries has been relegated to the bench permanently, as it were, due to his legs being blown off below the knees at Ypres. We did consider briefly for the plucky youngster to play in goal but ultimately the height disadvantage ruled against him. As to the second part of your question, frankly, a Somme offensive is news to me but we're always the last to know, first to find out, what? But I daresay it will all go jolly well, we've got Grinning Stümpfelpeiter on the run, no doubt about that. Now, if you'll all follow Private Wardell while the Hun reloads, he'll show you to your sleeping quarters. Still no takers on the night patrol? Ah well, don't say we didn't offer.'

Private Wardell led the journalists scurrying bent over double along the supply trench. Bullets whizzed overhead, stinging into the sandbags inches from their heads. 'Didn't any of you buggers bring a Red Cross flag?' grumbled McBride, wheezing from the effort.

'My boots will be ruined,' sobbed the travel correspondent as her leg sank again into the thick mud. She tugged it free and shrieked as she found her heel caught in the eye socket of a broken skull.

'Ah, Private Scott was wondering where that got to. He needed it at the time to try and keep his brains in. This way, ladies and gents, dinner will shortly be served in the drawing room,' said Wardell with gallows humour, gesturing them into a narrow dugout lined by bunks crawling with bedbugs.

'No reading lights, I see,' observed the chess writer from the *Guardian*. He wasn't quite sure what he was doing in Flanders, having found no evidence of chess activity anywhere. So much for the collection drive by the Women's Institute for strategy-based board games, he thought bitterly—waste, waste, nothing but tragic waste!

Wardell reappeared with steaming pannikins filled with a lumpy stew. 'And what are you serving this evening?' asked Prunella Fulton from *What's Cooking?*

'Remember that dead horse we passed this afternoon? This is his brother.'

Prunella shrugged. 'Oh well, when in Rome, do as the Romans do' she said and took a mouthful.

'Rome? I thought we were in France,' said Murdoch.

'It's a maxim,' said the man from the *Globe* drily. 'I daresay there's not much call for them in your stable of publications.'

'Only thing we need in our stable are a lot of good-looking fillies, preferably in their petticoats,' laughed Murdoch, smug in the knowledge that the lowest common denominator secured a return of the highest monetary denominations. Not that he would have phrased it quite like that. He was an idiot.

From the distance came a high-pitched whistle that gradually lowered in pitch to a howling scream before an almighty explosion shook the dugout, blowing the candles out. The journalists cowered in shock. 'What the hell was that?' stammered the shaken voice of the workers' struggle.

'Just Big Bertha letting one off,' said Wardell.

'How dare you insinuate such a thing—I resent that remark!' cried Bertha Mitchell, political correspondent for the Melbourne *Age* on an extended overseas junket.

'Sorry, love,' apologised Wardell, picking up his fellow Antipodean's accent. 'Nah, Big Bertha's a bloody great big howitzer Fritz has got parked behind his lines. Lobs over shells the size of pillar-boxes and there's not a lot we can do about it. You just don't want to be sitting on the karzi when one comes in—puts you right off, I can tell you.'

Setting aside her dislike of uncouth language, Harriet Warrington-Smythe surprised herself by asking a sensible question. 'What's it like for the men in the ranks?'

'Well, Big Bertha doesn't know if you're an officer or just a shitkicker like me and I reckon that's pretty much the case for the whole bloody show. Doesn't matter who you are, if the Bosch don't get you, the mud or the trenchfoot will. But this ain't too bad after Gallipoli—if you think the Western Front's all over the place like a lunatic's crap, you shoulda been in Anzac Cove. Total fuckin' disaster! Sooner they forget all about that shit-hole the better. Only trouble is, the peabrains that came up with that fantastic plan are the ones calling the shots over here! They couldn't win a pillow fight without half a million casualties. But maybe I shouldn't be tellin' you this stuff …' he said, suddenly cautious.

'Oh, no—you can trust us. We're journalists.'

'Alright. You seem like decent blokes. And sheilas,' he added with a grin at Warrington-Smythe. She blushed, already thinking of a three-page Short Fiction, 'Passion in the Poppies', the romantic tale of a young nurse in a field hospital falling for an injured larrikin from Sydney Town. Big Bertha broke her reverie.

'Sorry,' said Bertha, 'that *was* me this time.'

Wardell gave a laugh. 'Funny how you forget your inhibitions in a place like this. Knowing the next bullet might blow your head off, makes you kind of live life for the moment. You know the average life expectancy for a machine gunner in the front line? Fifteen minutes. You don't even make it to tea break. I'm surprised you've all lasted this long. O' course, this trench ain't at the sharp end but maybe you should be wearing these anyway,' he said, handing out some tin helmets.

They put them on and settled down for a night of tales of life lived on the line, chewing on Old Dobbin stew and listening to the dull thumps of artillery rounds and sporadic rifle fire. Gradually their ears tuned to the distant shells and they began to automatically stiffen when a change in tone indicated one coming that little bit nearer, bracing their backs against the damp earthen walls to absorb the shock of a close call. Their tongues loosened, their language coarsened and when Wardell broke open the bottles of cheap French cognac, they began to sing nostalgically for the ladies of Piccadilly, happily playing soldiers from the comparative safety of the rearguard trenches, before settling down to a hazy sleep, broken only by the bedbugs biting and the strains of reveille blown in the cold dawn light.

Bleary-eyed, they presented themselves to Major Looke before leaving to file their stories about the grim realities of war. They were surprised when Captain Dilley handed them each a typewritten page, variously headed with titles like 'Our Brave Boys' and 'War Being Fought with Drill-like Precision'.

'What's this, then?' asked the incredulous reporter from the *Guardian*. 'Don't tell me you're writing the stories for us?'

'Not me, I'm afraid. No, composition was never my strong point at school,' chuckled Major Looke. 'These come from the Press Liaison Office at HQ. I think you'll find they're all quite stylistically compatible with your various publications. No words of more than two syllables in yours, Mr Murdoch, and some interesting tips on looking good in khaki for you, Miss Warrington-Smythe.'

'Hang on a minute,' protested the *Globe* correspondent. 'I thought we were going to call the war as we saw it!'

'Come, come, sir,' said Looke soothingly. 'We may be thick but we're not completely bloody stupid.'

AD 1929

Buddy, can you
spare a zac?

The sun beat down remorselessly on Empire Street, a forgotten, grubby thoroughfare lined with dustbins, broken old fruit boxes and shattered glass that wound like a dead snake through Surry Hills. Hughie Flanagan staggered along under what little shade the mean terrace houses provided, his head pounding like a steam shovel from too much cheap plonk at Kitty Sullivan's pub. What was I thinking, he groaned to himself, mixing my varietal grapes? Shoulda just stuck with the verdelho. A good strong cuppa tea might put a lid on the pain but that meant sitting at the kitchen table under Ma's baleful look of disapproval. But he had to admit, you couldn't get a decent cuppa when you was out.

The front page of the *Mirror*, caught in an eddy of the hot westerly that had punished the city all day, danced across the lane and landed at Hughie's feet. The headline caught his eye: 'Wall Street Takes a Tumble'. Strewth, thought Hughie, I'm pretty sure I had a quid on that bloody horse in the fourth at Randwick! As he leant down and picked up the paper, the effort made him dizzy, so he sat in the gutter and forced his bleary eyes to focus. Nah, it wasn't about the nags at all. The stock market had crashed in New York and blokes were throwing themselves out of skyscrapers 'cos they'd lost the shirts off their backs. Hughie sneered—the one good thing about having nothing is you've got nothing to lose. But then he stopped, a worrying thought struggling to bubble up through the fog in his head. Stuffing the newspaper in his greasy pocket, he made for home with renewed determination.

'Don't think you're gonna get any sympathy from me,' growled Ma as she kicked the Kooka into life and put the kettle on the hob.

'Put a sock in it, woman,' shouted Hughie, rifling through the kitchen dresser for the household accounts. Betting slips, overdue gas bills and home-delivery menus fluttered to the floor until Hughie let out a cry of triumph and turned, clutching a page of scrip.

'What's that you've got?' asked Ma suspiciously.

'Me share certificate.'

'What are you doin' buying shares?'

'How else is a working man gonna drag himself up and pay for a self-funded retirement? If you want to keep your glamorous lifestyle when I clock off from the printin' shop, I've gotta have me investment strategy in place.'

Ma snorted as she looked around the sordid kitchen. 'You call this glamorous? 'Ere—you haven't been spendin' the money Dad left me, have ya? Them's the only savin's we've got!'

'Wisely invested in the stock market, my love. Buildin' a nice little nest egg.'

'Says here the stock market's crashed,' said Ma, brandishing the paper she'd taken from Hughie's jacket.

'That's in America, you drongo! Just shows you know nothin' about it—it's not gonna happen 'ere. We don't catch cold every time America sneezes.'

'Yes we do.'

'Do we? Well, I'll take your word for it even though thousands wouldn't. Makes no difference anyway—these are as safe as the Bank of England,' said Hughie, lovingly smoothing the creases from his share certificate. 'One thousand shares in BHP.'

'That's a good company,' conceded Ma grudgingly. 'Always be a market demand for minerals and steel-fabricated products.'

'Steel? What ya talking about steel for? This is BHP— Byron Heads Productions! They make pictures, bloody pillar of the local film industry, this is money in the bank, ya dozy sheila!'

The saucepan hit Hughie square between the eyes. When he came to, Ma shoved him out the door, protesting, to catch the tram into town and find out what the hell was going on at the stock exchange. Hughie had never visited the place. He'd bought his parcel of BHP shares off a bloke in the pub who was raising capital to make a feature after his first short film attracted a lot of interest, even from overseas. Or so he said. Anyway, Hughie had thought a remake of "The Kelly Gang" starring Chips Rafferty and Bud Tingwell sounded like a bonza idea.

Scraping in his pocket for the last of his loose change, he jumped on a rattler heading down Oxford Street to join the growing crowd of concerned small investors laying siege to the exchange on Pitt Street. On a nearby building, the chairman of the Rural Bank stood at the window ledge, threatening to jump.

'Can't have lost that much—he's only on the ground floor,' commented a thin bloke standing next to Hughie.

'What's goin' on?' asked Hughie, breathless.

'Whole market's gone belly-up, mate. Twenty-six per cent wiped off and that was just before morning tea.'

'You lost a lot?'

'Nah, mate. Saw it coming, sold everything yesterday. I'm basically your shark waitin' to circle in on the bargains.'

'Any news on Byron Heads Productions?'

'They just scraped the chairman off the pavement and took him away in an ambulance. No need for the sirens, if you catch my drift. Might as well wipe your arse with that for all it's worth,' said the stranger, gesturing to Hughie's share certificate.

'What about Empire Printing?'

The thin man laughed. 'Only thing they'll be printing are the redundancy notices.'

Head bowed, Hughie dragged his feet back to Surry Hills. He didn't even have the dosh for a tram fare. Ma greeted him with stony silence and a clout on the back of the neck with a frypan. That night, after a miserable supper of fried devon and the last of the wine cask, they held a family meeting. Lola and Delores sat either side of the table while Nanna huddled next to the oven, even though it was the wrong side of 90° outside.

'Your stupid father's gone and blown all our savings and he's lost his job,' said Ma.

'He's no father of mine,' mumbled Nanna, whose demented mind had her convinced she was an African princess.

'We know that, Nanna, you just keep chewin' your dog biscuits,' soothed Ma.

'How am I gonna pay for me trinkets and a night out at the pictures?' wailed Lola.

'Get a job like anyone else,' said her sister, knowing full well that Lola had never done a day's work in an upright position all her life.

'There's no jobs. I blame the government,' said Hughie.

'You always blame the government. Even when Lola had her trouble you blamed the government!'

'That's 'cos she got knocked up by the Minister for Housing!' shouted Hughie.

Ma shuddered, not wanting to remember the dreadful day when they'd sent Lola off to see Mrs Drake in Fortescue Street to get rid of it. She'd had to pawn her wedding ring to pay the old witch; it was the only thing Hughie had ever given her except a life of misery. She eased her aching back in the battered wooden chair—bloody osteopath was worse than useless.

'We'll have to go on the susso,' said Hughie. 'Fella I know down the pub says they're lookin' for left-handed shovellers to dig on the Sandy Hollow line.'

'You couldn't swing dixieland, let alone a shovel. Anyhow, you're right-handed.'

'I shovels and plays golf with me left,' said Hughie darkly.

'Maybe Father O'Reilly at St Bridget's will help us,' suggested Delores.

'Take charity?' gasped Ma with immovable Irish pride. 'I'd sooner die! But we could try nicking the sacristy candlesticks, they'd have to be worth something. Too late for the rent, though—Mr Hooker's comin' first thing in the morning.'

'I'll take care of him,' scoffed Lola.

'Well, just you be careful. We don't want another trip to Mrs Drake.'

'What, you think I'm givin' it away? He's not gettin' a Number Ten for one week's rent on this renovator's delight in Surry Hills, I'm not that stupid.'

'We haven't paid the rent for six months.'

'Bloody hell,' said Lola, thinking of the job ahead. 'There goes the cyclin' holiday!'

The next morning, as they sat on the pile of their meagre posessions out in the street, Lola kicked sulkily at a tin can.

'Not my fault he were a pansy.'

'Don't look at me,' said Hughie as Ma turned on him.

'I can't say I'm not a little curious but there's some things I draw the line at.'

'How can they do this to the heiress to the throne of Mozambique?' muttered Nanna.

'Nothing for it, I'm afraid,' said Hughie, drawing himself up. 'We'll have to go on the wallaby. Try our luck out bush.'

'But we'll be starved of culture,' wailed Lola, who could've wailed for the Olympic team.

'Aw, come on, Lo, it might be fun. See the animals and that,' said Delores.

'Mate of mine down the pub says they're looking for fruit pickers down the Riverina. Probably the only chance I'll get of putting my hands on a nice pear. Ow! What the bloody hell was that for?' cried Hughie.

So, bickering and grumbling, they left Nanna with a note tied round her neck to fend for herself, and trudged up to the Pacific Highway to cadge a lift going south. Realising their mistake in Taree, they cadged a lift with a lorry driver heading for Victoria, and sat perched amongst the mangoes and star fruit destined for the gourmet fruit shops of Toorak. After he'd dropped them off on the far south coast near the border, they stowed away on a boat headed for the riverland. Realising their mistake when they reached New Zealand, they cadged a lift on a tramp steamer and wound up at the mouth of the Murray, where they headed nor-east, begging for odd jobs at farmhouse doors. Lola soon found the farmers were more interested in other types of jobs and she handily kept the family's fortunes afloat until, in late 1930, they reached an orchard outside Mildura.

'We're lookin' for a bit of work,' said Hughie, cap in hand, to the farmer who eyed them suspiciously through the slightly open front door.

'Not students, are ya?'

'No, mate. We're from Sydney, down on our luck.'

'They got fleshpots in Sydney. I been there twice. I was tempted and fell, it's a wicked town!'

'Why'd you go back then?'

'I had to make sure. Are you in the union?'

'Er … should we be?'

'No red union labour on this orchard, strictly enterprise bargaining on a contract-by-contract basis.'

'No worries, mate, as long as we get a fair day's pay for a fair day's work.'

'Beggars can't be choosers. Start at dawn. You can doss down in the cowshed.'

'Thought this was an orchard.'

'You telling me how to run a farm, city slicker? I keep three heifers for tax purposes, if you must know. And I don't want 'em upset, alright?'

And with that the door slammed shut. The Flanagans wearily plodded to the cowshed where the heifers looked at them in alarm, wondering if this was the midnight knock on the barn door that meant a one-way trip to the pet-food factory. Ma looked around, shaking her head sadly.

'Never thought I'd think of Empire Street as a palace. You don't know what you've got till it's gone.'

'Yeah,' said Lola, 'when you're goin' backwards, standin' still looks pretty good.'

'Cheer up, Ma,' said Hughie, feeling a rare pang of affection for the old girl. 'We'll get back to the Hills one day, you'll see.' He struggled to get his arms around her.

Ma clipped him over the ear. 'Don't even think you've got a chance, sunshine. I haven't forgotten Armistice Day.'

'Leave it out, Ma. Let's get some kip, I'm done in,' said Delores, kicking off her worn shoes and dropping onto the hay where she fell asleep at once. Hughie looked at her, tears brimming in his eyes—and he hadn't even been drinking. I dunno, he thought, a cove tries to do his best, raise his kids right and the world just backs up and wallops him—there's no bloody justice in a long-overdue market correction. And with that he settled himself down to sleep, narrowly avoiding a steaming cowpat.

The next day in the frosty dawn the farmer led them to a grove of straggly fruit trees.

'I want all these out. I'm going upmarket, putting in grape-vines.'

'In a depression?' asked Hughie incredulously.

'Still on with the farming advice, eh, city boy? You think everyone's suffering like you? Depressions don't touch the toffs. They just sit on their capital and wait till the storm blows over. Plenty of land going beggin' for anyone cashed up, you can buy labour for a quarter the price of last year and still have change to buy your fancy goods, your wine, your washed rind cheeses and so on.'

'You seem to know a lot about it,' said Ma.

'I read it in the Bible,' said the farmer defensively.

'Don't seem right when millions o' blokes are scratchin' for a feed,' said Hughie.

The farmer shrugged. 'I don't make the rules. God fashioned a hard world. Look at the animals, they don't curry no favours. Sure, you make things easy for the pretty ones, but it's dog-eat-dogmeat in the long run. Depression's just like a drought but it only hits the poor buggers without a big enough tank. Now, enough of the commerce lesson, I want these trees out by sundown.'

Grumbling, the Flanagans set to work. They were joined by a motley bunch of dossers and battlers who'd somehow got a sniff of the work on offer, men and women from all walks of life down on their luck struggling to keep their heads above water. Delores sawed the half-rotten branches, Ma went at the trunks with an axe, pretending they were Hughie's head, while the object of her long-lost affection swung the mattock, breaking up the rocky ground to grub out the stumps. Lola broke a fingernail and had to go and sit down to recover. Lunch was a slab of damper and thin tea and there was no let-up until the sun fell behind the mallee.

Back in the cowshed that night, Hughie sidled up to Ma.

'Ma, me luck's changin'. I met a bloke down the orchard today, he's got a sure-fire tip for Flemington.'

'God's oath, Hughie Flanagan, are you never gonna learn?' cursed Ma.

'This is a dead-set cert for the Melbourne Cup! All I need is bit of dough to put on it.'

'After all you've put us through? It's not enough that you've lost your job, the savings, your daughters are livin' with three heifers in a cowshed—not to mention me with my delicate chest. We can't sink much lower but now you want to blow the rest on a horserace?'

'Aw, give us a break, Ma. A bloke tries to hold down a decent job and what happens? The bloody bosses fold like a pack o' cards at the first sign of trouble! He tries to do the right thing and invest for his future—and give a local industry tellin' our stories to our people a bit of a leg-up in the process—and the whole thing blows up in 'is face. They get you comin' or goin', Ma, you gotta take your chance when life's bitin' you on the arse. Seems to me like the whole thing's a gamble at the best o' times. So I was thinkin' if you handed over your …'

'Oh no, Hughie. You can forget that! You're not getting me brooch, the only thing I've got to remind me of my Da, 'specially seeing we've had no word from Nanna.'

'But this is our big chance to get back on our feet! When this little beauty comes in, we can go back to the Hills with our heads held high, maybe I could get a job with the council or somethin'. Bosses like a man with the smell o' winner all over him.'

'You're dreamin', Hughie. Face it, the bosses have got us just where they want us and it wouldn't make a scrap of difference if you went in there smellin' like the Pope. Besides, if I had a quid for every time you've told me you had a dead-set cert, we coulda bought the bloody council by now!'

Hughie sighed, turning the scrap of paper the tipster had given him over and over in his calloused hands. 'Yeah, you're right, love. Who am I kiddin'? Blokes like me are just scraps floatin' on the ebb tide of history, he said reflectively—and he hadn't even been drinking. 'Bloody nag'd probably come dead last. Have to, when you think about it, with a stupid name like that.' He tore the paper into bits and threw them in the straw. 'Phar Lap to win? Ha! Buckley's and none!'

AD 1962

East of the wall

Snow descended gently on the cobblestones of Gewürtztramminerstrasse, the cascading ice particles held briefly in the blinding shaft of a searchlight then left as suddenly to fall in darkness as the beam swept on in its endless patrol. Berlin sank ever deeper into winter, her still-damaged streets and shattered buildings softened by the mantle of dirty grey snow, save for the Wall that ran like a livid scar through the city, dividing East from West. Along its twisted concrete and barbed wire course, the snow had been swept clear and watchtowers gazed out across a sterile canyon that few dared cross.

Just off the street, hidden from prying eyes around the corner in Achtungschnellstrasse, an ageing Skoda stood parked by the broken kerbstones, its engine ticking over, snarling and backfiring in protest at the weak mixture of diesel and used vegetable oil it was being fed. The left indicator didn't work too well either, the brake pads were all but worn away to nothing and the nearside wing was rusted out like a pumice stone — how it got through rego was anyone's guess.

Not that roadworthy compliance was much on the mind of the car's sole occupant, a heavy-set Russian far more concerned with coaxing what little heat the engine produced into the cabin to counter the bitter cold. Dimitri Bytyerbolockov struggled to read the Skoda manual by the flame of his Zippo cigarette lighter, sole souvenir of his one meeting with Allied forces east of the Elbe in the dying days of the First World War. Well, there had been candy but he'd wolfed that down within five minutes and the silk stockings had laddered the first time he'd worn them. But the trusty Zippo had never failed him, even though the imperialist lighter-fluid blockade made it harder to refill.

Grunting, he forced the obstinate levers into position to demist the windscreen and warm his feet, then gently nudged the accelerator to increase the idling speed with a deftness that belied the twenty-six stone he carried on his sturdy Georgian frame. Raised on a diet of cabbage, black bread and hazelnut spread, Dimitri had boxed heavyweight for the Red Army and few who had met his left hook approaching at speed ever wanted to risk meeting it again. But hooks can be deceptive; he was in truth a gentle giant, preferring the solitude of books to the conflict of the boxing arena. He'd finally hung up his gloves after accidentally knocking a referee into a coma; mortally ashamed, he'd simply walked away weeping from the ring.

His had been a tough war. Eight months in Stalingrad with no sign of his ring improving, and even though he'd been transferred out long before the Germans reached the city, his job in the quartermaster's storeroom had been quite tiring. Leningrad was even worse; the stores were in complete disarray, nobody knew where anything was, and as the Nazis relentlessly pounded the city, Dimitri had taken it upon himself to catalogue the entire boot collection single-handed. His organisational skills did not go unnoticed. He'd been summoned to Moscow in '44 to work in the Kremlin library, getting the stack into some kind of user-friendly shape. Then, when the Red Army stormed into Berlin to finally smash the fascist myth of a Thousand Year Reich, Dimitri had travelled west to assist in the repatriation of any Soviet prisoners still left alive. From there, he'd drifted into the intelligence services, working his way steadily up through the ranks of the KGB, fighting the undeclared war against the forces of imperialist capitalism. So far he'd risen to Special Corporal, a unique rank conferred on him by a management team that didn't really know what else to do. What do you call a secret-service operative of fifteen years standing with badges in Unarmed Filing, Alphabetisation (Cyrillic) and Coded Dymo Labelling?

Since being posted to East Berlin as the Wall was going up in '61, Dimitri had worked in the decoding section, sifting through the mountains of intercepted radio messages from the Allied sector (most of them pizza orders) and encoding top-secret instructions for Soviet operatives deep in the West (most of them duty-free orders). Then only last week, a particularly nasty virus had swept through the station and practically all the staff had come down with it. Dimitri had so far, touch wood, escaped infection and was mightily glad he had—his comrade Yiroslav from the motor pool said it was the worst congestion he'd ever suffered, he could hardly breathe at all during the night and his gums really hurt. The sick absentees had left the service critically undermanned, so when Moscow had dropped on them the last-minute rendezvous with a CIA agent, Colonel Smirnoff had little choice but to give Dimitri the job.

'No heroics, Bytyerbolockov,' the Colonel had sniffed, nose rubbed raw by endless coarse paper towels, pride of the Soviet facial tissue industry. 'This is a preliminary meeting about prisoner exchange, nothing more, nothing less. Just find out the time and the date they want to do the swap, okay?'

Dimitri had saluted briskly, almost knocking himself out in his anxiety to look sharp. At last, he'd thought on the trolley bus home—this is why I joined the KGB! Well, apart from the pension plan and the canteen. As soon as he'd reached his solitary flat in a prefabricated block on the city's outskirts, Dimitri had revised his vernacular English, a curious patois cribbed from a pile of cowboy-and-western comic books sent by a pen-pal from Utah in the days when such contact was encouraged.

And now, as he sat in the Skoda waiting, Dimitri again wondered if 'varmint' was the sort of word you could safely use in a formal situation. Wiping the fog from the driver's window, he looked across the street as two drunken East German soldiers came lurching out of a doorway. These people were always drunk. Alcohol consumption outside licensing hours was an offence but he decided to turn a blind eye. He had far more important business at hand, the thought of which had his stomach muscles tensing in apprehension.

A soft tap at the passenger's window made him jump. Checking in the rear-view mirror to ensure the soldiers were out of sight, he leaned over to wind down the window but the handle came off in his hand. Adding that to his mental list of vehicle defects, he opened the door.

A slight figure, his features unrecognisable beneath the layers of clothing that swaddled him, climbed into the car, cold vapour steaming from his mouth. He sat, staring straight ahead, then began to sing softly in a tuneless baritone, 'Well, since my baby left me, I've found a new place to dwell.'

Dimitri blinked hard and cleared his throat nervously. He hadn't sung in public since summer camp on the Black Sea. 'It's down at the end of lonely street,' he began in a key that was frankly too high for him, 'called Heartbreak Hotel.'

There was a silence. 'That ain't strictly correct,' said the

American, glancing nervously out the side window. Dimitri was puzzled. He'd practically worn out his bootleg 45 of the King singing his signature ode to loneliness; he was sure they were the right words.

'You shoulda sung "at" Heartbreak Hotel instead of "called" Heartbreak Hotel. That was your mistake but I guess we can let it ride.'

'I am thinking we have established the recognition criteria,' said Dimitri in stilted English. He bashed the gear shift and with a grate of complaint, the Skoda moved off along the dark street. Both men stayed quiet, unsure of what to say. Turning into the Burgherkönigplatz, Dimitri ventured a conversational gambit. 'Have you in East Berlin been often visiting?'

'First time through the checkpoint. Kinda nervous.'

'On the left,' said Dimitri, trying to put his guest at ease, 'we are the Criminal Courts of the People's Tribunal passing.' Putting his guest at ease? He was placing the verb at the end of the sentence and he wasn't even German! Calm down, he thought. 'And on our right side, you can be seeing the Indoor Volleyball Centre of the Glorious Soviet Revolution.'

'Where the Dresden Cossacks beat Kiev Dynamo 21-18 in the third last Thursday,' said the American.

'You follow indoor volleyball?' asked Dimitri, amazed.

'Nah, I intercepted the wire sending the results to Moscow.'

'Top-secret information, no?' said Dimitri, smiling.

The American laughed. 'Well, I guess if you're a Dynamo fan it's kinda sensitive material.'

Then, remembering their ideological divide, they fell silent. Dimitri drove to the suburb of Praline-unter-Lindt, where the KGB ran a few safe houses to conduct operations independently of the Stasi. Before the war, its gracious mansions had been home to wealthy German industrialists but even now, seventeen years after the fighting stopped, nearly all the houses remained empty, ruined shells. Still, it was handy for the shops. The Skoda came to a juddering halt outside a gatehouse and after a quick look around to make sure no-one was following, Dimitri led the American inside.

The finest Soviet workmanship had left the place still looking like an abandoned wreck but there was a solid fuel stove burning warmly in a corner and a bottle of vodka sat temptingly on the table. Grabbing two glasses, Dimitri gestured for his counterpart to sit on the roughly upholstered easy-chairs. Probably more comfortable on the floor, thought the Russian as he tentatively lowered himself onto the horsehair, but the CIA man didn't seem to notice, perching himself on the edge of the chair and tapping his feet nervously on the floor. He took the offered shot of spirit and drank it neat.

'Might need another just to take the chill off,' he said, wiping his mouth.

'No problem, quickdraw. Hi-yo, away!' answered Dimitri. The American gave him a queer look but said nothing. 'So, we are to organise a rendezvous. We give you one of yours, you give us one of ours.'

'Seems kinda weird, doesn't it? We play this whole deadly cat-and-mouse thing then just turn up for a swapmeet.'

Dimitri's eyes narrowed. Was he being set up? He wouldn't be the first to fall for the sting of mouthing counter-revolutionary thoughts to a bogus operative. He knew the KGB set such traps with hidden tape-recorders; he'd typed the transcripts in triplicate himself.

'Hey, ease up, big fella,' chuckled the American, reading his mind. 'I ain't carrying a wire. Search me, if that makes you feel better. But could you warm your hands up first?'

Still uncertain, Dimitri poured another vodka.

'You been in this game long, comrade?' continued the American. 'Pretty new to it, myself.'

'I have been a servant of the Soviet people for many years, er, pardner, working for the liberation of the international proletariat.'

'What's that? Some kind of insurance firm? Hey, don't sweat it, I'm just pulling your leg. I know who your international proletariat are, I been translating reams of that stuff ever since I got here.'

'You speak Russian, Tonto?' asked Dimitri, surprised.

'Heck, yeah, but I ain't gonna try it now, not when I got a chance to be talkin' to the Lone Ranger! Where'd you learn all that Tonto thing?'

Dimitri blushed. 'I had pen-pal in Utah. He send me literature. But why they assign this mission to you, a junior?' he asked, sensing that perhaps Colonel Smirnoff had not been entirely honest about the importance of this assignment.

'We had this god-awful virus in the section, just about wiped everybody out. Real bad sinus congestion, some got the gastric thing with it. I was the last one left standing.'

'Same here,' said Dimitri with a grin, reaching for the vodka bottle.

'Seems like germs don't recognise the Berlin Wall, huh?'

'Bad flus travel fast,' said Dimitri, delighting in his new-found ability to pun without a cowboy reference. 'But we should get to business.'

'No rush—I don't get safe passage back through Charlie until dawn. So seeing I've got a real live Russkie sittin' here in front of me, I'm gonna ask you this: what the hell d'you want to go and build that wall for?'

Dimitri snorted. 'If you had US army, nuclear bombs, B-52s all pointing at you from twenty metres, you would not want to protect yourself?'

'Sorry to break the bad news, comrade, but barbed wire ain't gonna keep out the B-52s, even if they was flying real low. See,

I reckon it's all about keepin' people in, rather than keepin' people out.'

'Why? They have no reason to leave,' said Dimitri, knowing he wasn't being entirely honest. He himself had always harboured a secret desire to see Dodge City.

'Don't get me wrong—I think you Russkies have done a hell of a lot, what with the war and everything. Twenty million casualties! I mean, even allowing for bad management that's a mighty sacrifice. And you've got people into space, you figured out the bomb, your peasants have food on the table. But they don't have freedom, they got to have permission just to cross the street! And your Kremlin's shit-scared they're gonna want to cross to the sunny side! My fight ain't with you, comrade, it's your system.'

'And yours is better? Black man slave in his own country, millions live in poverty, Dick van Dyke show recommissioned for third series? What, poor man free to travel to Honolulu? Pan Am going to give him ticket for nothing?'

'Well, no. But he's got a choice. If he wants to work real hard, he can get anything he wants.'

'Not so easy, I don't think! The workers are oppressed, living on tips. Look at Cisco Kid—he has nice horse, Pancho just gets silly hat. In Soviet Union, citizens make sacrifices for each other. We build a nation for all, not just work for personal frequent flyer account.'

'Look, I take your point about Pancho but you gotta remember he's probably an illegal citizen, you don't know who's coming over the border from Mexico.'

'Maybe you should build wall,' said Dimitri pointedly.

The American ignored the dig. 'But let's say Pancho gets his green card and he's not Stateside just for the welfare benefits. If he wants to pull himself up, make a name for himself, he can do it. That's what your free market does, comrade. If he wants to start up a riding-school, or a western adventure ranch or go diggin' for gold, no-one's gonna say he can't.'

'Except man who owns all the land in Wyoming, or gold mining company who bribes senators for licences, or big multi-national riding school concern,' protested Dimitri, basing his argument on a hazy recollection of an editorial in *Pravda*.

'But your free market makes room for everybody!'

'Yes—plenty of room for failures, pretty squeezy at the top!' Dimitri snorted with contempt. Either that or he was coming down with the virus. He topped up their glasses and threw another log into the stove.

'Okay, but no rule says you can't make your own space up there,' said the American. 'Let's take burgers—you have burger stores in your country?'

'There is government department of burgers. Controls whole chain of stores, many with walk-through facility.'

'So you've got the one choice for your burger. Now, are you telling me that in the USA, we'd stand for one burger company just takin' over? That one, or maybe two, burger companies are gonna rule the market in hamburgers all over the world? I don't think so! Let's take freedom of the press.'

'There can only be one truth; it only needs one press.'

'I don't know about that, a man's got to be free to say what he thinks.'

'Tell that to Senator McCarthy.'

'Hey, fight fair, big buddy—I didn't vote for him! But I can't see every newspaper, radio and television station in the States—and there's gotta be hundreds of 'em—gettin' taken over by a handful of proprietors. People wouldn't stand for it! The free market ain't gonna let someone just waltz in and buy up every network and tabloid and start tellin' people how to think— that's not gonna happen. You ever hear about computers?'

'Of course. I have diploma in punch cards.'

'I've got a few buddies in the computer game, and they're tellin' me that one day, everybody's gonna have a computer sittin' on their desks. Sounds crazy I know but that's what they're sayin'. Miniaturisation is what they call it.'

The American suddenly reached into his pocket, pulled out a dog-eared snapshot and offered it to Dimitri. It was a grainy photograph of a young boy, awkwardly pulling a red wagon along a pebble dash driveway.

'That's my boy, Bill Jnr. Turned seven in October. You think what the world's gonna be like when he's our age. Colour television, men flyin' in space every day, maybe even world peace. And your computer's gonna be a part of that. It's gonna set people free, open up a whole new world. Now your Kremlin wouldn't want a bar of that, they'd be losin' control. But your free nations are gonna run with it! And can you tell me that one, or maybe two, big companies are gonna corner the market? No, sir! Anybody can have a part of the computer industry, anyone can grab a piece of this pie.'

Dimitri shrugged. 'A cup of coffee is just a cup of coffee, makes no difference who sells it. Point is who is able to buy it.'

'You can get coffee anywhere you choose in America, forty-two flavours. Joe Average can just go out and buy himself a diner, make coffee, sell a few sandwiches and put his kids through college. No way that's gonna change. You Russkies centralise, we diversify. I can't see a time when there's one big fat coffee conglomerate snappin' up every diner and pushin' their own kinda beans. That's not how it works and that's why, my friend, you can build your wall as high as you like but you're never gonna stop people wantin' to crawl over the top.'

'To each according to his needs,' said Dimitri flatly.

'Well, maybe some of us just got a hungrier kind of needin'.'

'It's the fat pigs who empty the trough. Who looks after the runts?'

'It's a tough old world out there. Now,' said the American, draining his glass, 'I hate to turn to business but about this exchange: here's what we're offering.'

And so the conversation turned to dead letter drops, contact points and unmarked vans. The long night wore on, and eventually they dragged the chairs before the stove, settling to fitful sleep beneath coarse woollen blankets. As the pale light of dawn struggled to break through the heavy cloud cover, Dimitri coaxed the Skoda back to life and they drove through streets deserted but for the occasional trolley bus and heavily clothed worker struggling on the icy pavements.

Checkpoint Charlie stood bathed in artificial light. The guard examined Dimitri's identity card and letter of authorisation before staring hard at the man in the passengers seat. Finally, he gave a curt nod and waved them through the barrier with his machine pistol. They sputtered a short distance to the wooden hut from where the American would be escorted back to the Western Sector. Dimitri killed the engine before it could expire of its own accord.

'Well, it's been a pleasure to meet you … I don't even know your name,' said the man from Washington, shaking hands.

'Dimitri. Dimitri Bytyerbolockov, Special Corporal and Cultural Adviser, KGB.'

'Don't make it so long next time, Dimitri.'

'When we can agree to disagree again, *kemo sabe*?'

'Right. And don't forget what I told you about computers. They're gonna change the way we run the world on both sides of this goddamn fence. Every man his own boss.'

The American got out of the car and walked towards the waiting military escort. Dimitri wound down the driver's window. 'You never told me your name,' he shouted.

'Gates,' said the American, turning. 'William Gates II. Hi-ho, Silver, away!'

Not quite the end
of the world

The muted chatter in the Scout Hall faded altogether as Brian entered from the kitchen door and led the committee up to the dais. He waited for the last of the latecomers to settle themselves then cleared his throat and banged his open palm on the table.

'Right, I'd like to call this extraordinary meeting of the Millennium Doomsday Cult to order. Proceedings commenced at … 11.30 and the date is January 3rd …'

'2000,' came a dry voice from the second row.

Choosing to ignore the pointed tone, Brian continued. 'Do we have an agenda, Denise?'

'Well, no,' stammered Denise, a diminutive woman who had recently given up her job as a clerk with the roads authority. 'I mean, none of us thought we were going to be here, did we?'

'I believe that was part of the mission statement,' needled the dry voice.

'Look, Garry,' said Brian, unable to turn a deaf ear any longer. 'Have you got a problem?'

'Yes, I have, as a matter of fact. My problem is that as of

midnight three days ago, we were supposed to be embarking on the celestial mother ship for a better life—nay, paradise— beyond this universe but unless I'm very much mistaken, we're still in Arncliffe.'

'What's wrong with Arncliffe?' said someone, somewhat missing the point.

'Nothing at all,' said Garry. 'Nice little suburb, handy for the CBD, with rising property values but according to our illustrious leader the place is meant to be a smoking ruin by now and the only persons with a passing interest in the real estate should be the Four Horsemen of the Apocalypse. Which reminds me—anyone caught sight of the Antichrist?'

There was an embarrassed silence. Neil, formerly with Parks and Gardens, coughed nervously and spoke. 'I thought I spotted him at the autobank but it turned out to be that bloke from *All Saints*. You know what it's like, you see a famil- iar face and can't place it ...' he trailed off feebly.

Brian could sense things were getting out of hand. Trou- blemakers like Garry were poison, asking awkward questions and eating all the cream biscuits. Discipline was the one thing you needed in a cult—well, apart from the absolute certainty of blind faith, and if anyone knew that it was Brian; he'd lost count of the number of cults he'd been closely involved with ever since his parents divorced two years before he was born. (At least that's what his grandmother had told him and as a small child, he had believed everything she said. After all, she was twenty-four.)

Brian polished his glasses deliberately. Not that he needed prescription lenses but spectacles made him look older and wiser, another handy cult tip he'd picked up along the way: people always seem to put their faith in the short-sighted. He sighed importantly and spoke with authority. 'I think we should move on to the financial report.'

Cult treasurer Stanley, five foot-two in his Bata strides with the elevated heels and handy compass, had, with an accountant's innate sense of caution, held onto his job at H & R Block. Not that he hadn't believed that the world would come to an end on the stroke of midnight but after his deep personal disappointment with the Bhagwan some years ago, he'd been understandably nervous. He shuffled to his feet to speak.

'Well, there are one or two outstanding membership dues. I think some members, I mean particularly those members with dues falling last November or December, might have thought twice about paying,' he said with a half-hearted laugh. When no-one shared his humorous insight he quickly moved on. 'So I'll pop those down on the credit outstanding side. We did incur a penalty for premature withdrawal of our term deposit but in accordance with the committee's wishes, the remainder was incinerated on the steps of Parliament House as a protest against the corrupting stain of Mammon. We've, er, received a bill for cleaning up the mess—normally I'd pay it out of petty cash but that all went on the Astral Voyage Garments.'

'Astral Voyage Garments?' snorted Garry. 'Bloody fancy name for tracksuits—you could've bought them from Target at half the price we paid on the stupid bloody internet!'

'Language,' muttered Mavis.

'I suppose we could attempt another fund raising raffle,' said Stanley.

Brian looked doubtful. 'We didn't sell many tickets last time.'

'Small bloody wonder!' came the by-now-predictable interjection from Garry. 'First prize was a Christmas-in-July weekend! You're hardly likely to buy a few raffle tickets to leave in your will on the off-chance, are you?'

'Well, maybe we could on-sell the cyanide pills,' stammered Stanley.

'Sorry—I ate mine,' said Neil. 'Thought it was a Vitamin C.'

'Well that's just bloody typical, isn't it? We can't even buy decent suicide pills!' said Garry exasperatedly.

'It got rid of my cold, though,' replied Neil matter-of-factly. 'Just as well, too—I didn't fancy the idea of astral travelling with post-nasal drip.'

'We could try for a refund from the manufacturer in California but I'm not sure if they have a customer complaints department,' offered Stanley, his mind racing through the tax implications because he'd claimed the cyanide pills as a legitimate business expense. The cult was registered as a church for tax purposes and this year's return was already completed and in a shoe box under his bed, to be opened by his mother in the event of his removal to another spiritual plane.

Brian rose to his feet ominously. 'Look, forget about the cyanide pills. Can we please keep our minds focused on the big issues?'

'We haven't had a seconder for the financial report,' whispered Denise, prodding him with an HB.

'Not now, thank you, Denise. Listen, people, I'm talking about our eternal salvation here. I'm talking about the path from darkness to glorious daylight that was promised in my vision—promised to you, the faithful who have remained true and courageous. Frankly, I'm a little disappointed by Stanley's news about the lapsed membership fees, but I have a heart that can find forgiveness. Can you look into your inner being and say the same of yourself? Okay, we've had a minor setback …'

'Minor setback!' cried Garry. 'Jesus wept, that's like saying Goliath managed a commendable second!'

Brian ploughed on. 'But cast your minds back along the difficult path we've trodden together. Remember how deflated we felt when the Godhead did not appear to us in 1988?'

'We did get to see the Tall Ships—that was a bonus,' said

Neil, trying to be supportive.

'Exactly. Even from loss comes consolation. Halley's Comet; alright, major disappointment. You could hardly see it, even with really good binoculars. And I know some of you were angry when the eastern seaboard didn't collapse during the last solar eclipse as I predicted it would.'

'They had mud-slides at Ulladulla. Not your fault the council wouldn't listen to you,' said Mavis.

'Thank you, Mavis. Your belief only strengthens my resolve.'

Mavis blushed. Little did Brian know she'd optimistically packed a double sleeping bag to share with him on the long trip to Alpha Centauri. Having known no-one intimately in this life, Mavis was determined to not miss out on love in the next.

'But let me ask you this question,' continued Brian, oblivious to the waves of secret passion emanating from the fourth row. 'How many years in a millennium?

'A thousand—look at today's calendar!' shouted Garry.

'And when the first millennium began, did anyone bother to record the Year Nought?'

Garry opened his mouth to say something then stopped. Puzzled frowns appeared on faces; Neil looked simply baffled.

'No, my friends, they did not. And likewise, we left it from our calculations. I have indeed foreseen the end of the world but anticipated its arrival prematurely. But logic tells us the new millennium will dawn ... when?'

Nervous looks were exchanged but no-one offered an answer.

'Fourteenth March?' offered Neil tentatively, seizing on the date because it was his mother's birthday and he had often hoped for the world to end when he invariably forgot.

'No, brother. We leave this life when the next millennium truly begins: in the first minute of the first day of the year 2001.'

There were astonished gasps from the audience. Garry muttered something incomprehensible.

'So patience, my friends, patience. Maintain the faith,' concluded Brian rather smugly as he sat down and made a show of looking through some important papers. An audible sigh of relief ran through the hall.

'Right. Any other business?'

'I'm probably jumping the gun,' said Denise. 'But has anyone had any thoughts on a venue for this year's Christmas party?'

AD 2001

The road to Kabul

'Charlie!' cried Brigadier Parker as he crossed the foyer of the Department of Defence building towards an elderly gentleman struggling to rise from his chair. 'I've haven't seen you for, gosh, how long is it?'

'Strike me lucky, I've never had any complaints from the missus so it must be long enough!' said the wiry senior with a grin.

Parker chuckled politely. Charlie Warner had been an army entertainer all his life and even now, though long retired, he couldn't resist the trademark wisecracking that had made him a legend of the AIF (Light Ent Division). Twice decorated in the Far East for gallivanting under fire and awarded an MBE for services to the double entendre, Charlie now spent his days in a rest home on the Gold Coast, where he kept those residents who weren't in a permanent vegetative state entertained with his lively bingo calls. And it was only recently that the doctors had put a stop to his Thursday Smokos on the grounds of pulmonary health and safety.

Parker walked to a door and punched in a security code.

The door opened in automatic silence and he ushered Charlie through then led him down a long corridor filled with earnest-looking people in military uniform carrying important files from one office to another.

'You've done alright, sir,' said Charlie, whistling in appreciation. 'Top brass in Canberra, all very much at the pointy end. And to think I met you when you were a pup fresh out of Duntroon still wet around the ears.'

'Lot of water under the bridge since then, old boy.'

'Too right—not long till I'm washed right out to sea!'

'Oh, there's life in the old dog yet. You'll see us all out, Charlie,' laughed Parker, opening an office door and gesturing him in. 'Would you like tea? Do you have one lump or two?'

'Two, last time the doctor looked!'

Parker laughed uncertainly, unsure if Charlie was obliquely referring to his genitals or a potentially life-threatening medical condition. He sat down at his desk while Charlie pulled up a chair, looking around the office admiringly.

'Very nice, but I don't suppose you've asked me down here to admire your prints. So what do you want with an old retired trouper like me?'

'Well, Charlie, this is strictly between you and me, we don't want the media getting hold of this. I don't know if you're aware of the war against terror …'

'Oh, they do give us newspapers in the old folks home, sir. Usually laid over the floor in case of accidents but I keep up with the news.'

'Quite. You probably know that this country's put our hand up and joined an international alliance in Afghanistan, providing logistical support, covert operations, the usual stuff. But we've also been asked by ALPHA B-FOR HQ to lend a hand with morale, entertaining the troops on the ground and what have you. That's where you come in.'

'Strewth, why me? I'm a bit long in the tooth, ain't I?'

'Not at all. The government is keen to retain active senior citizens in the workforce and your knockabout brand of entertainment is a dress circle ticket to a golden age that few of us will see again—just the thing for a lonely soldier far from home. All very well to have the internet and satellite TV but nothing beats a familiar face and a topical reference. Besides, we have your Centrelink details and know where you live.'

'Crikey! Volunteers step forward and that's an order! Don't worry, Nosy, I'll pack up the old kitbag and do me bit. When's kick-off?'

'First things first, Charlie. Our Variety Liaison Officers need to clear your material. It's an internal procedure we put in place after Vietnam—the department didn't want a repeat of the Little Patty "It's Time" fiasco at Long Pok. I'm sure you understand.'

'Too right—in triplicate! Don't lose sleep, Double, I'll dot the t's and cross the i's. Cross the i's—you with me?'

Parker laughed politely.

'So what d'you think the lads'd like to see?' continued Charlie, rummaging through a bag of old scripts that never left his side, even when he slept. 'My skit as Private Parts or Major Bumsore? I've got a beaut cross-talk routine between a Gippo trader and the quartermaster ...'

'Er, yes ... fact is, Charlie, things are a little delicate. It's a very broad coalition fighting the axis of evil and we have to make sure we don't inadvertently offend any of our allies.'

'So who's on our side?'

'That rather depends on the day of the week. And to make things more difficult, we're not entirely sure who's on the other side either.'

'Ah! Double agents, secret transmitters, French Resistance, that type of caper?'

'Well, in a way. Half the current enemy were the former resistance but that was back in the days when half our current allies were our former enemies ... you know the way it goes Charlie, it's all politics.'

'And that's a rum game that a cove can do without! So lay off the wogs and go easy on the fuzzy wuzzy gags, is that what you're saying?' said Charlie, mentally combing his back catalogue for jokes that didn't target an ethnic minority. 'Looks like a job for Corporal Punishment and the waitress from Armentieres. Blokes can't get enough of a French maid outfit— "Tart for dessert, monsieur?" Solid gold, that is.'

Parker coughed nervously. 'Women play a vital part in today's armed forces, probably best not to demean them—we don't want the Equal Opportunity Commission on our backs. Perhaps something a little more contemporary ...'

'Say no more, squire. Sophisticated audience, eh? Working blue, all continental stuff!'

Brigadier Parker sighed and walked to the window. He'd marked this down as a bad idea from day one but relations with the Minister's department were frosty to say the least; they'd wanted Vera Lynn and the surviving members of the Glenn Miller Big Band but no-one could find the money for the medical support teams. He'd made a counter-offer of Human Nature and the Minogue sisters but to no avail. The Minister was determined to make the military campaign against terror look like the sort of war we'd had in the old days. We'll be digging air-raid shelters in the back yard and handing out ration books next, thought Parker bitterly. And why? The Hume Highway posed a greater threat to the lives of Australians than al-Qaeda but someone smelt votes in a war without end and was going to play the whole thing to the hilt. And who was he but to do his masters' bidding?

Turning back from the expansive view of besser bricks, he

spoke. 'Our good friends the Americans are providing their own units, it seems their troops have trouble understanding anyone else. Although I believe they're having the devil of a job finding a replacement for Bob Hope. So we'll be liaising with the entertainment divisions of NATO. The Germans are sending an oom-pah band on the strict proviso that it's only used defensively—there's still a member of the Wermacht Merry-Makers under investigation for war crimes committed in a Belgian beer tent in 1940 so they've been understandably rather sensitive about deploying entertainers in a strike capacity overseas. The French are being typically uncooperative and have only offered us Monsieur Bippo. Honestly, he's older than you are, Charlie, and can't do the white-face because of his eczema—I really can't see the point of having him at all but there you go. Good news is, the Brits have recalled Colonel Dartmoor to put together a gang show.'

'Binky Dartmoor? Stone the crows, I haven't seen him since the Malaya Insurgency! He's a laugh and no mistake—the best Margaret Rutherford impersonator ever to work the Far East. He played twelve weeks at Souths Juniors in the late '60s, packed the place out eight shows a week. Bloody good man to have behind you when the chips are down and you've got a ten-o'clock matinee. I can still remember his monologue closer ...'

Before Parker could stop him, Charlie launched into the joke.

'This bloke walks into a pub and says to the barman, "I'll have everything you've got on the top shelf." The barman looks surprised but he starts pouring. So the bloke has the gin, the scotch, the champagne—Dom Perignon, the good stuff—the Drambuie and the tequila, he downs the lot in one go. Then he wipes his mouth, burps, and says to the barman, "Ooh, I shouldn't have had that with what I've got." And the barman says, "Why, what've you got?" And the bloke says, "A dollar fifty."

Charlie laughed till the tears were streaming. Parker wondered if this was the same sort of mental torture the terrorists used to motivate their suicide bombers. He suddenly had a nightmarish vision of Charlie dressed as Gladys Moncrieff reciting the punchlines from saucy postcards to a group of Northern Alliance fighters on a snowy scree in Afghanistan.

'Yes, very good,' he said resignedly. 'Alright Charlie, I'll send you your embarkation details as soon as we have the flights arranged.'

Charlie wiped his eyes and looked at Parker, blinking in confusion. 'Flights? Am I going somewhere?'

'Why, yes. You're going to entertain the troops in Afghanistan, remember?'

'That's not on the Gold Coast, is it? Who are you, anyway? This doesn't look like matron's office,' said Charlie, bewildered.

'Charlie, it's me,' said Parker, somewhat alarmed. 'Brigadier Parker.'

'Sorry, squire. I wouldn't know you from Adam. I think I've had one of my funny turns.'

Parker closed the file with a mixture of sadness and relief. He gently helped Charlie to his feet and led the confused octogenarian to the door. 'Never mind, Charlie, there's been a bit of a mix-up. We'll get it sorted and have you home as soon as we can. Did you bring your medication with you?'

An hour later, Parker gave a half-hearted wave to the departing ambulance and walked back through the automatic doors into the foyer. A vaguely familiar figure sat waiting. The brigadier consulted his file then walked briskly over to the new arrival.

'Ah, Mr Farnham, good of you to come. Now, tea? Do you have one lump or two?'

AD 2002

The real meaning
of Christmas

'laus, S.,' cackled the Tannoy. 'Claus, S!' it barked more
impatiently. Santa blinked out of his doze, heaved
himself up from the cracked plastic chair he'd occupied
for the last three hours and made his way to the counter,
ferreting out his papers and Job Seeker Diary from a grubby red
trouser pocket.

The officious goblin behind the glass security interface
leafed through them with an air of disdain. 'Not many inter-
views in the last ten months.'

'I'm a seasonal specialist,' apologised Santa. 'Things always
look up around Christmas.'

'Don't try seasonal with me. I had the Easter Bunny in here
last week. He'd done a course. Picked up some promotional
work and three months part-time in phone sales. But he's got
the right attitude, self-motivated, get up and go.'

'All that sugar, no doubt.'

'Nothing to do with sugar. It's what's he's got up here,' said
the goblin testily, tapping his head.

'What … fur?' ventured Santa.

'Always the quick comeback, isn't it, Claus? A rabbit tries to make something of himself, stand on his own two feet …'

'Hardly a major achievement given the size of them.'

'… and you have to look down your nose, Mr All-the-World-Loves-Santa Bloody Claus! Well, let me tell you something, my friend: the world's not handing out the free lunches any more and pompous tubs of lard like you are going to find out the hard way.' He stamped the papers with an angry thump and shoved them back across the counter. 'And thank you for accessing North Pole Community Services.'

Santa sighed and made his way out, standing aside as an anxious family of elves came in, caps in hands. A sharp wind blew from the north, or from the south, depending on which side of the street you were on, and a thin sleet settled in his beard. There hadn't been a decent snowfall in months—something to do with global warming, according to the Tooth Fairy, but he hadn't been completely reliable since the introduction of fluoride. Pixies and reindeer trudged through the sludge, heads down, and a group of vacationing penguins consulted their copy of *Let's Go Arctic Circle* with grim determination.

Catching sight of himself in a shop window, Santa paused for a closer inspection. Short, ruddy and overweight, in spite of the diet which Mrs Claus had clipped from a magazine (no carbohydrate in the morning; no protein in the afternoon). My God, thought Santa, I look a hundred years old. Which cheered him up slightly, because he was at least a hundred and fifty. He ambled on to the post office to pick up the morning's mail but his private box was worryingly devoid of anything except a pamphlet offering discount carpet cleaning. Where were the pleading letters from children the world over? Every year he was getting less and less and the few that did arrive were filled with increasingly unfathomable requests. He'd never heard of

Intravenous Barbie. Oh, for the days of Matchbox cars and tea sets—or better still, hoops. Hours of innocent childhood fun and one elf could knock out a thousand of them in a shift. But the golden age of the hoop had died with Queen Victoria, Santa grudgingly conceded, and for children today it wasn't enough to simply be alive for another Christmas. Ungrateful sods.

When he arrived home for lunch, Mrs Claus greeted him with ominous news. 'We're on a different diet,' she said. 'Bran Nu U, it's called, been on the best-seller list in Greenland for six months. You'll never guess—it's bran-based. Helps you to unleash the power within.' Santa had never needed much help in that department but nonetheless he sat down to eat and together they ploughed their way through bran fillets served on a bed of bran with a glass of bran juice.

'Community Services rang for you,' said Mrs Claus when she'd cleared the last husk from her throat and her eyes had stopped watering. 'Seems you've been causing a bit of trouble again. They want you to talk to a Career Re-orientation Operative.'

Santa merely grunted.

'New rules, they said. You've been reclassified as casual, so you've got to look for other work. Six weeks of benefits from Boxing Day then that's it. And Leslie the Elf has handed in his notice. Says he can make more money in phone sales. We'll be short-staffed.'

'We've always been short-staffed. Elves are short,' said Santa.

'Please, San, be serious,' said Mrs Claus, her voice catching and her eyes brimming with tears. Santa gave her a whack between the shoulders and a bran-flake flew from her mouth and across the room. 'Two of the reindeer have got foot-and-mouth,' she continued when she got her breath back.

'Not Rudolph!' cried Santa.

'What are you talking about, you silly old thing? Rudolph

was put down five years ago—a merciful release, the vet said. If that red rash had spread any more he'd have looked like a sun-dried tomato with legs. No, it's the two with names no-one can remember.'

'Doona and … er …'

'Well, whatever they're called now, we won't even be calling them for breakfast soon. I tell you, I don't know how much longer we can keep going.' Mrs Claus stacked the plates. 'Branuccino?'

'Not for me, dearest. Think I might check my emails.'

Not that it will do much good, thought Santa as he staggered upstairs to his study, lunch rumbling threateningly in his stomach. Santaclaus.com had been registered as a domain name by a pedophile network in Holland; Father Christmas and HoHoHo were now trademarks owned by the Disney corporation. Occasionally he received a message addressed to his derivational root 'santeklaas' but they were invariably from bookish, socially challenged loners asking with a sense of detached irony for Tolkien calendars or this year's collection of *The Far Side* cartoons.

He logged on to the cheap computer he'd bought in a car-boot sale. Nothing, except for an offer of discount carpet cleaning and ten free minutes in Gobblin' Goblins. Wasn't technology a wonderful thing, he mused; selling answers to problems that didn't exist and providing a whole new way for people to fall out of touch with each other. Sighing deeply, he turned to see Mrs Claus standing in the doorway.

'Any messages?' she asked nervously.

'None. I fear the only children who still believe in me are preliterate and their parents, carers or state-appointed guardians are apparently reluctant to write on their behalf. Or should it be behalves?'

Mrs Claus's face clouded with worry. Sarcasm never sat well

on a stout person. 'You mustn't blame yourself. After all, childhood is a nineteenth-century invention.'

'As indeed, largely, am I,' said Santa resignedly. 'If anyone wants me, a) I'll be surprised and b) I'll be in my grotto.'

She watched him plod down the stairs, heel flapping where the Tarzan's Grip had again failed to repair his left boot. The computer put itself to sleep and as she looked at its blank, accusing screen, a tiny idea began to form in her head.

Weeks later, on the morning of Christmas Eve itself, Santa sat before the Careers Re-orientation Operative. The operative was himself a Re-Tooled Dwarf, as he put it, and had made the switch from mining to life consultant after attending a self-motivation workshop. 'It changed my world,' he smiled. 'Shifted my focus. Believe in myself, I can believe in others. I believe in you, Santa—well, not in the traditional sense, I stopped believing in you when I was seven. Which is funny when you think about it because here you are.'

'Hilarious,' said Santa.

'But I want to believe in the new you. No, seriously. Let's face it, what future is there in the past? Time was when everyone pinned up the stocking but who bothers now? Kids know where the presents come from, they're not stupid.'

'It's never been just about presents,' protested Santa. 'I see myself as a symbol of universal goodwill, a benevolent provider of happiness …'

'I'm afraid it's Wiggles one, Santa nil in that particular ball-game.'

'I'm the last bastion of innocence, gatekeeper between childish wonder and the disillusioned self-interest of adult-hood.'

'The self-centred gene kicks in prenatally these days—they've done the tests to prove it. About the only thing that's better to give than receive is a boot up the arse,' said the dwarf, shuffling his papers and bringing that avenue of conversation to a close. 'So. What are we going to do with you? Toy manufacturing's moved off shore, much cheaper to churn out the stuff in South-East Asia. Santa's Helpers went onto enterprise bargaining and nearly all the ones with valid working visas negotiated an exit package, while the rest were packed off back to Nova Scotia or Lapland to the arms of their loving families. The reindeer rebate scheme's been scrapped and Santa's Grotto has been placed in the hands of an administrator. I think we can safely say the days of leaving out a glass of milk for old Saint Nick and a carrot for Rudolph have gone the way of the long-playing record. Fair assessment?'

Santa remained silent, his head bowed.

'Options. Relatively few, I'd hazard a guess. Not much call for sleigh drivers, though having your own sack might come in handy if we go down the postal service path. Your weight issues send the price of worker's comp in a skyward direction, employers prefer someone under ninety years old and your skill base wouldn't get you into high school.'

'You're enjoying this, aren't you?' murmured Santa.

'Not at all. Just being pragmatic—not sure if that word's in your Cloud Cuckoo Land dictionary but in the real world it comes between outmoded and profitable. So ... I think a call centre should suit you right down to the ground. Report to this address—let's see, today's Christmas Eve,' said the dwarf as he perused the calendar. 'I'll be reasonable. You can report there tomorrow. And thank you for accessing North Pole Community Services.'

Thoroughly depressed, Santa wandered off to the post office to close his private box. No point in keeping it on now. Swinging back the little door for the last time, his eye fell upon an envelope addressed in a childish scrawl. He seized it and ripped it open, fingers trembling. 'Daer Santa,' it read in a curiously familiar hand. 'I am five yaers old and want a bycixle for christmas. and a pirat ship and a playstashun. and a hoop. no Harry Potter, i am over him. plese come to visit me and all the kidz who think you are the bestest even tho they don't wright and tell you, the ungreatful sodz. love virginia.'

Santa looked at the letter in disbelief, his eyes brimming with tears. Fumbling the post office box closed, he pocketed the key and hurried home with new-found energy. He burst through the front door and called to his wife. 'Mrs Claus! A letter!'

'A letter?' said Mrs Claus, feigning surprise as best she could.

'Yes—addressed to me! From a child! Quickly, we must pack the sleigh, I leave at midnight. I tell you, my dear, there's life in the old legend yet!' he cried, beaming as he strode towards his grotto, bellowing orders to a surprised Leslie and the other ancient elves waiting to retire on full super.

Mrs Claus smiled to herself. Well, well, well. A letter. Anything is possible, she thought, quite simply anything, as long as *someone* believes in you.

For an alternative ending in tune with today's lifestyle, read on!

Santa's trip ended when he was intercepted by ADI officials, and four thousand chimneys on the eastern seaboard were retrospectively excluded from the migration zone. He was arrested and interned for processing at the Port Hedland facility. His sack was destroyed by Federal police in a robotically detonated explosion and the reindeer were put down by Customs officials fearing an outbreak of HADAD, or Human Acquired Deranged Antler Disease. The Federal Government issued travel warnings for polar exploration and hinted that they couldn't rule out a possible wave of allegorical characters landing illegally. Mrs Claus was denied access to her husband, despite the protests of her agent and the intervention of the civic rights group Barrister for Humanity, which was later dissolved, as one legal-aid solicitor is technically neither a barrister nor a group. The film rights to the story were acquired by Jan Chapman but investors lost interest when Santa hanged himself in his holding room. Despite accusations of poor taste, Channel 9 went ahead and screened 'Santa You Old Poof—The Celebrity Roast' hosted by loveable larrikin Eddie McGuire.

AD 2047

Space:
the final chapter

Flight Captain Mike Sattler nudged the retros to ease the shuttle orbiter's speed and toggled the comms switch to the open position. 'Mission control, this is *Esperanto* requesting clearance for final approach to space station *Terra Nullius*.'

There was a silence, broken only by phasing static then a short burst of ambient music. A digitised voice spoke in a flat, neutral accent.

'Your communication is important to us. Please hold and your enquiry will be answered by the first available Mission Control operative. For atmospheric re-entry, press 1. To counter-check your remaining fuel supply, press 2. To return to the main menu, press 9.'

Sattler sighed and gazed out the window. Way down below him the earth seemed to slow as the shuttle approached geo-stationary orbiting speed on its regular transport run to the massive space station that sat majestically 300 km above the equator. The synth and shakuhachi music stopped abruptly and a real human voice answered from the Mumbai control centre.

'Sorry for that delay but we copy your request, *Esperanto*, we are currently processing you for docking through portal 7-1-hash-9.'

'Roger and Denise. 7-1-hash-9'

'Would you like this directive reissued in any of the following randomly selected languages: French, Mandarin, Portuguese or Hindi?'

'Negative, Mission Control.'

'Did you pack your own bags? Are you or any of your crew carrying fruits, nuts or plant products?'

'Er … that's an affirmative and a negative.'

'Have you recently visited any agricultural installations or come in contact with any livestock in the Asia-Oceanic global quarantine quadrant?'

'That's a negative, Mumbai.'

'Are you or any of your crew now, or have you ever been, members of the Communist Party or the German National Socialists prior to 1945?'

'Ah … I'm going to have to check that, Control.'

Sattler flicked the comms switch to internal. 'Heads up. Any of you blokes ever been in the Communist Party?'

The headphones rackled into life. 'Commander, I'd just like to remind you that there are women on board and that not all of us identify as "blokes",' said scientific officer Li lin Ng sternly from the depths of the cargo bay.

'My apologies, Officer Ng,' said Sattler, silently cursing his mistake. The slip of the tongue probably meant two hours of on-line gender bias counselling. 'Was anyone a Nazi before 1945?'

'Give us a break, Captain! I don't want to appear ageist but that was a hundred years ago,' chuckled astrophysicist Oscar Davies, a burly American from Boston who identified person-ally as an Afro-Caribbean Non-Indigenous American Gay/Queer Vegan.

'Well, I've got to ask the question.'

'Excuse me, Captain,' came a voice in halting English. Sattler recognised Doc Mi Pai, an elderly bioethicist from Shanghai conducting deep space experiments on the neural pathways of depressed gerbils. 'I was briefly member of Boys Brigade after Cultural Revolution.'

Sattler frowned; any delay would have them missing the docking window. 'I think we can overlook that, Professor Pai.'

'Are you sure that's wise?' asked Dr Primakov in a disembodied voice from the sickbay.

Bristling, Sattler muted the comms and turned to the only person on board he could trust, Second Officer Brian Harvey, a fellow Sydneysider. 'Bloody rich coming from a Russian,' grumbled Sattler to his 2IC. 'I know they got rid of the Communist Party over fifty years ago but I reckon it's in the blood.'

Harvey grinned. It was only because Oceania held the rotating chair of the UN Space Station Control Commission for the 2046–8 triennium that two crew members from Australia had been allowed to fly the same mission.

Sattler reopened the intercom. 'Time is pressing, Dr Primakov, and I'm confident that Professor Pai's admission does not contravene the spirit of the Station Access Convention, in particular the US-initiated sub-clause 23c.'

'I think we should put it to the vote,' said Primakov.

Sattler groaned in frustration. Sometimes the democratic process was a real pain in the butt, but ever since the catastrophic collapse of the global economy in the Greater Depression of '23, there was little alternative. When the sharemarket disappeared up its own dividend, the private sector had been effectively wiped out and the world reorganised into five economic governance zones coordinated from the United Nations headquarters in Beijing. A new international constitution had been drawn up by delegates at the Delhi Convention in '28 and now all political and trade ties between the five zones were governed by its exhaustive regulatory procedures—the preamble alone was in three volumes. When *Terra Nullius* had been sent into orbit from Canaveral by the Cubans who now controlled what had once been Florida, it went aloft as a world project and was technically under the control of the central body so negotiations between the five member zones were often protracted and difficult.

'Okay, we'll put it the vote. All those in favour of me exercising the commander's discretionary powers to ignore Professor's Pai's admission?'

There was a chorus of assent over the comms.

'And those against?'

Silence.

'Dr Primakov, I thought you wanted to vote?' said Sattler exasperatedly.

'I did vote. I changed my mind. Democracy in action, no?' said Primakov with a chuckle.

Wise-guys/girls, thought Sattler, who needs 'em? He initiated the docking manoeuvre and sat back to let the onboard computers log onto *Terra Nullius'* mainframe via microwave link. Through his window he could see hatch 7-1-hash-9 opening like a lotus as the engagement arm of the lander eased forward towards it. A sight of sweet precision that never ceased to enthral him, it was hard to believe that the linkage hardware had become a major issue for the engineers when Europa lodged an objection to the male/female symbolism of the procedure. 'Virtual rape of the mother ship' was the description forwarded to mission liaison by a concerned gender ethics committee in Finland and for months the designers had vainly sought a way to connect two craft orbiting at 30 000 kmh without any kind of phallic symbolism. Eventually the impasse was broken by an enviro-poet from Thailand, who pointed out that certain types of worm practised self-coitus and the connection of two spacecraft, being other-worldly, could be regarded as the yin and the yang of one organism reuniting within the self. Muttering, the Finns had reluctantly agreed.

Once Sattler and Harvey had overseen the safe transfer of scientific crew and cargo, they made their way to the canteen. The sustainable organic food had all been prepared by a kosher halal vegetarian butcher. Each carrot had first been given a chance to run away and then plucked from the earth at dawn before being julienned facing east. The lactose-tolerant drank their milk confident that the cow had given it willingly and the tofu had been blessed during an ecumenical mass. Obesity and heart disease now being recognised as fundamental human rights, burgers, fries and pizza were served in a discrete airtight pod adjoining the main dining area, and it was here that the two Australians sat, somewhat guiltily, chewing on quarter-pounders.

'So, who are we taking back?' asked Harvey between mouthfuls.

Sattler pulled a list from his pocket. It was printed in eighteen languages, braille and pictograms for the illiterate. 'Sensitive cargo, mate. There was a bit of a stoush between the Irishman, the Scotsman and that Latvian from Human Resources so the ombudsman's been recalled for counselling. Seems she didn't follow complaint procedures.'

'But we didn't bring up a replacement,' said Harvey, puzzled.

'They're going to try a new approach. Role-playing restorative practice, increases empathy and leads to natural justice apparently,' shrugged Sattler, draining his generic World Cola. He suspected it was Pepsi long past its use-by date but without a blindfold he couldn't be sure.

Harvey looked around to make sure they were alone. Video surveillance was unlikely, contravening as it did the right to privacy enshrined in the Constitution, a clause that had killed off television current affairs and, in Harvey's personal opinion, some pretty good websites. 'I heard,' he whispered, 'that it's because she isn't a lesbian.'

'Could be why she's on the outer,' conceded Sattler. 'But that bloke in microbiology—you know, the transgender Irian Jayan—he told me she's two months behind in her performance targets and hasn't done her feedback matrix forms since she got here. That's the stuff that's going to get you in the end.'

'You're probably right,' said Harvey, unbuckling his restraint. 'Now if you'll excuse me, I've got to see a person about a quadruped.' He floated off through the hatch in search of the unisex toilets.

Sattler flattened his fries carton for recycling and returned his plates to the servery in consideration of others. They weren't scheduled to depart for another thirty-six hours and he had little to do apart from a debrief with the *Terra Nullius* commander. Might as well get it out of the way, he thought, and made his way down the long corridor that separated the amenities wing from the administration block.

Admin was by far the biggest section of the space station— the legal department alone took up three levels and the media relations centre another two. Commander Mugawe, or Principal Team-leader as she preferred to be known, had her office right at the heart of the sprawling ship. 'My hatch is always open!' she liked to say, secure in the knowledge that double-entendres had been banned under the Vanuatu Protocol. Paralysed from the waist down in a debating accident, Mugawe was the first ability-challenged African woman to run a space station. Others had commanded shuttles and orbital landers but she was the first to take control of *Terra Nullius*, where zero gravity rendered her wheelchair irrelevant, and she enjoyed the respect of her multinational crew.

And little wonder—hers was a challenging job. The anti-discrimination laws handed her a team that currently ranged in age from eighty-six years to eighteen months—this was the first spacecraft in history with long daycare. *Nullius* boasted a synagogue, a mosque, chapels of all the Christian denominations, a Shinto temple, a Buddhist cell, a small room for the worship of Satan and an equal opportunity pod for atheists. The unisex facilities catered for three gender types—or four, depending on which angle you were coming from. English was the official station language but that was only because New Zealand (now the richest nation on earth thanks to the discovery of vast deposits of heliozircoluminum just north of Waitangi) had insisted. In certain sections of the orbiting behemoth, alcohol was banned; in others, it was positively encouraged. Smoking was only permitted outside but a few die-hards still braved a spacewalk every two hours for a quick gasper.

Mugawe waved Sattler into her office. 'Greetings, Captain. Pleasant trip?'

'Pretty uneventful. We've brought the new microbe-generators for the self-replicating wheat experiment and I believe you requested chocolate,' answered Sattler, grinning.

'There are some things a brave new world should not be without, Captain, although rest assured I shall keep it in tight quarantine from the nut-allergic. And I hope you remembered the latest series of *Home and Away*—it's never the same via broadband.'

Sattler produced a small crystal from his backpack. 'It's all on there, all 758 episodes.'

'Extraordinary, isn't it? I can remember a time when you'd need two of those to store that much. Well, pleasantries aside, what news of home?'

The Captain paused. His shuttle was one of three that serviced the ship on a monthly basis, each based in a different earth zone. Tensions had been growing for some time now between the US and the Latin American Federation that stretched from Tierra del Fuego in the south right up to what was left of California after the devastating earthquakes of '36. The US had been pushed back into the eastern states and even though a shadow of its former powerful self, the concentration of wealth and vengeful hostility remained an destabilising influence in world affairs. The whereabouts of much of its nuclear arsenal remained a mystery and fears were growing in Asiana and Europa that renegade patriots had seized control of some truly awesome firepower. Unsure of where Commander Mugawe sat in the shifting political allegiances, Sattler was circumspect.

'Surely you're kept aware of all developments,' he offered politely.

'Officially, yes, but things are so different on the ground. Shuttle crews are my eyes and ears.'

'Well, the situation's tense in the Americas. China's staying on the sidelines but there are reports of sabotage in the Middle East, maybe pointing to some kind of US-initiated activity.'

'Who cares about the Middle East? Ever since oil went the way of the horse-drawn cart they've had about as much international influence as Tonga! So they've cornered the world market in sand, big deal.'

Sattler was taken aback; this was loose talk for an officer of Mugawe's seniority. And she was ability-challenged, he thought, talk about your glass houses! Secretly, he believed the obsession with not offending anyone had itself become offensive—but those were thoughts best left to the privacy of one's own mind. Mugawe saw the uncertainty flicker across his face.

'Forgive me, Captain, but sometimes the straightjacket of international love and harmony gets a little too tight.'

The awkward silence was broken by a pulsing alarm and a light flashing urgently on the console. The Tannoy burst into life.

'Commander, we have a situation. We're getting strong radioactive disturbances interfering with terrestrial communications. *Nullius* has lost contact with Mumbai.'

Mugawe swung into her command chair and tethered the restraint. 'Any luck from the back-up earth relay stations in the Pacific?'

'Negative,' continued the comms officer. 'I don't know how to say this but it looks like the whole network's taken a series of EMPs, like it's being hit by a wave of small shocks—but I can't see that happening without some kind of major energy disruption …'

'Don't be ridiculous, you'd have to be talking nuclear activity at least,' Mugawe interrupted sternly.

Sattler was staring through the porthole at the earth far below. 'Commander, I think you should see this.'

The steely urgency in his voice brought Mugawe quickly to the window and she looked down to see the globe's fragile atmosphere being punctured by shock waves swirling around epicentres dotted over its whole surface. Her face froze in horror.

'Holy Christ!' she whispered, briefly forgetting Clause 37c(i) of the Station Code of Conduct prohibiting blasphemy against any of the world's religions. 'That's a nuclear fucking war!' There went 37c(iv).

'What?' said Sattler, not wanting to believe it but knowing something had gone terribly wrong.

'Well what the hell else can make upper atmospheric disturbances like that?'

'Could be bursting weather balloons?' offered Sattler, very

desperately clutching at straws.

'Tactical thermonuclear devices, Captain, that's what.'

'But deployment is banned under the Wangaratta Protocol!'

'Maybe whoever's letting them off didn't read it,' she snorted, pulling herself with her powerful arms back to the control console. 'I want this station locked down, alert status chartreuse with potential escalation to watermelon.'

'Watermelon?'

'It's a pinky red but a red with yellow in it, you know what I mean? Don't blame me, a committee from San Francisco chose the international threat status tone palette.' Mugawe opened all internal communications channels. 'Sorry, but I don't have time to do this on the email, okay? Engineers, I need a power status check asap and shut off all non-essential electrical systems until we figure out what's going on down there. All medics to man or woman each triage station in every sector—you do not, I repeat not, require proof of St John's First Aid certification with you, this is not an exercise, people. All scientific personnel to secure laboratories and suspend research until further notice and please, don't forget to back up, we may experience power surges.'

No sooner had the words left her lips than *Terra Nullius* lurched violently.

'Holy fucking crap!' shouted Mugawe, really burning her bridges this time, especially as she had an open mic in front of her. 'They've started dropping the big ones, this has gone strategic! Do you know what this means, Sattler?'

'Holiday leave is cancelled?'

'Well, yes, but worse than that—*Nullius* won't be able to keep her orbit. The shock waves are either going to send us spiralling into the earth or flying off into space.'

Sattler thought fast. 'Not necessarily, Commander. We've got two shuttles docked—we can push her—sorry, it—away and restabilise in a higher orbit when the explosive pulses are spent. Let's face it, they can't go on much longer.'

He trailed off and they looked at each, his words dropping like stones.

'They said it could never happen,' murmured Mugawe. 'Rogue missiles triggering a tactical response, warhead deployment escalating until no-one knows where they're coming from, critical mass reached and the strategic reserves engaging automatically. That's what has happened, Captain. You're right. It will be ended soon.'

'It will all be ended, Commander. There will be no earth to go back to.'

They fell into silence. Sattler's stomach lurched, his mind unable to contemplate the enormity of what had happened. He stole a glance at Commander Mugawe as she gazed unblinkingly at the earth tearing itself apart, her strong cheekbones melting under the tears that slowly fell from her limpid eyes, broad shoulders straining against the thin fabric of her thermal skivvy as her firm breasts heaved against the waves of emotion shuddering through her. Sattler felt a stirring in his space suit.

Mugawe suddenly turned to him, a strange and distant gleam in her eye. 'But is it the end, Captain? Those below us may perish yet we still live. *Terra Nullius* has escaped unscathed and pushed to a higher orbit, she—sorry, it—can continue to shelter us for many years to come.'

'What about food?'

'With care we could survive on our reserves for a year— eighteen months if we don't have dessert every night. And we can grow more food in our laboratories.'

'But we have little water …'

'We can recycle our own waste.'

'Sounds attractive,' muttered Sattler.

'Captain, we will all have to make sacrifices. I know I should wait for a full report and some kind of analysis but you know as well as I do that the horror we all thought impossible has been unleashed on earth. Mankind has chosen to destroy itself but God, or whatever other-ness you identify with, has chosen us to carry humanity's torch. Has chosen us to survive and return to re-people the planet when the desolation has passed.'

Re-people? Sattler's space suit began to stir almost uncontrollably.

'Think of it, Captain. This ship contains a representative of every race and creed on earth, man, woman and child. The smartest technology, the greatest science and I think there's a copy of Shakespeare in the library. The finest minds, the strongest bodies, tempered by those among us less than perfect: the physically challenged, the emotionally less stable who find relationships difficult. What better nursery in which to raise a new civilisation, freed from the prejudices and petty rivalries of the past?'

She gazed at Sattler, a smile fleeting across her trembling lips, her eyes glistening as she struggled to keep her emotions in check. Sattler held her gaze as the *Terra Nullius* sailed on through the void to an uncertain future—a feeble bastion of humanity.

Free from prejudice and injustice? Jeez, he thought, she might be right. And I tell you what, she might be a crip but I could be in here!